The River in Winter

The
River
in
Winter

new and selected essays

STANLEY CRAWFORD

UNIVERSITY OF NEW MEXICO PRESS

ALBUQUERQUE

A number of these essays first appeared in *American Way*, *Double*, *High Country News*, *Land and People*, *The Santa Fean*, *The Smithsonian*, and many northern New Mexico publications.

Library of Congress Cataloging-in-Publication Data

Crawford, Stanley G., 1937–
   The river in winter : new and selected essays / Stanley Crawford.—1st ed.
     p. cm.
   ISBN 0-8263-2857-1 (cloth : alk. paper)
   1. New Mexico—Social life and customs.   2. New Mexico—Rural conditions.
   3. Water—Social aspects—New Mexico.   4. Country life—New Mexico.
   I. Title.

F801.2 .C73 2003
978.9—dc21

                  2002152216

DESIGN: Melissa Tandysh

To Gus Blaisdell

CONTENTS

A number of these essays were written under a grant from the Wallace-Reader's Digest Fund, which also provided the time to rewrite and assemble them into a book. Others were written during residencies at the Villa Serbelloni of the Rockefeller Foundation's Bellagio Study Center; at Centrum in Port Townsend, Washington; and in Marfa, Texas, as part of the Lannan Foundation's residency program for writers. Without the generous support of these foundations, this collection might never have seen the light of day.

Many of the shorter essays first appeared in the *Santa Fean Magazine* as installments in my column, "Fifty Miles North." Wolf Schneider, my editor there for two years, has my deep-est thanks for guiding me to backyard and down-at-the-river topics, including the title essay. Susan Bergholz, my agent of seventeen years, stimulated a steady flow during the prior era, and Beth Hadas of UNM Press was instrumental in gathering them up between two covers.

Now comes a longer yet no less important list of friends and relations who have served as sparks, minders and reminders, interlocutors, supporters, questioners, goads, and critics—the essential tool kit of any writer who does not (whatever the occasional illusion) work in the utter solitude of another planet. There is no hierarchy here except for one, my wife Rose Mary, who stands at the top of my list as first reader and editor, and our children Adam and Kate, essential members of both the stage crew and cast. To them, I add: Elsie and Bernie Aidinoff, Dorothy Andrews, Esteban Arellano, David Benivides, Sallie Bingham, Diane Boyer, Steve Brugger, Gallilee Carlisle, Mark Childs, Walt Coward, Steve Davies,

ACKNOWLEDGMENTS

Miles and Susan Davis, Clark DeSchweinitz, Brian Drypolcher, Jaune Evans, Greg and Yolanda Fanslow, Harvey Frauenglass and Gayle fulwyler Smith, Robert and Caroline Grant, Sarah Grant, Ted Harrison, Paul Hawken, Susan Herter, Sam Hitt, Mike and Ellen Johnson, Phil and Rose Kaufman, Fred Kent, Ray Kingsley, Alice Klaphake, Van Klaphake, Zita Klaphake, Esther Kovari, Ernie Larsen and Sherry Milner, Joe McElroy, Helen MacLean, Kathy Madden, Deborah Madison, Malcolm Margolin, Donald Meyer, John and Lyn Pohlmann, Lynda Prim, Nausika Richardson, Steve Robinson, Benjamin T. Rogers, Tom Romero, Pam Roy, SueAnn Snyder, Lee Swensen and Vijaya Nagarajan, Robert Templeton and Karen Cohen, Alison Tinsley and Chris Fields, Bob and Becky Tracy, Alice Waters, and Steve Whitman.

I BRIEF HISTORIES

|1999| As a straight line person who has settled in a crooked line region, I think a lot about lines. About how the seventeenth-century Spanish colonists, our first real estate developers, drew lines across the landscapes of New Mexico to lay out the boundaries of their land grants, lines that defined and enclosed their communities to be. About how, starting with a bend in a stream or a river and a brush and rock dam, they must have coaxed tongues of water out toward higher ground, letting the water find its own contour line, then etching and digging the damp earth with sticks and poles and wooden shovels, painstakingly excavating the first acequia channels in those sites where the Pueblo Indians had not already done so. Given the crude instruments and tools of the times, and the purposes for which they were drawn, few of these lines would have had any need for geometrical straightness.

And then how, in the 1880s, the straight line people arrived, with their squares and rectangles and sections, and their steel rails and wooden cross ties and taut-strung telegraph wires—and how they completed their work by introducing that most revolutionary form of the straight line, barbed wire, which was invented in 1874. And how the straight line people also carried with them an elaborate philosophy of private property, the wire, upon which they had strung a whole system of laws, the barbs, which even animals had to respect.

There are two ways lines have been drawn in Northern New Mexico, to two purposes: one, to draw a circle, to enclose a community, much in the way an acequia flows out away from the stream or river and then arcs back to it; and, two, to section up

3

the land in angular grids for the purposes of quantifying property, the better to speculate in it or market it.

There is of course another way, a primordial way, the way that nature draws lines: the edges formed by streams and rivers, ridges, escarpments, mesas, and lines of vegetation that shadow contours of geology and altitude, and the tracks of creatures and the trails of men and women on foot that interconnect campsite, spring, forest, meadow, and river. It is to places like this we go when we wish to escape our own too straight and too confining fences, and the sharp pointed barbs of our quantifying civilization. Much of my fascination with acequias lies in the way that these man-made watercourses have drawn vegetation and wildlife out away from their river sources, turning the channels into almost natural structures, like overgrown ruins.

By heritage I am a straight line person descended from perennial Anglos who colonized Ireland, Ontario, and finally Southern California. But by the time I got to New Mexico with my wife Rose Mary from another colony—Australia—and other roots—Irish-Italian—the colonizing gene was fatigued, needing to be colonized itself, seeking the softer, enclosing line of community. Certainly the barbed wire fence is universal now, but in the little river valley where we have lived for over thirty years, to those tending the acequias of the valley or fishing the river, barbed wire is merely a physical obstacle, not a philosophy with the power of law behind it, or not quite yet. "No trespassing" signs are still rare in our adopted valley and are considered vaguely insulting or rude to the more egalitarian sentiments of humankind, like gated communities.

But even though the straight line seems to have carried the day, all those other lines lie hidden or half hidden beneath our feet, beneath our tires, beneath the pavement. Between Santa Fe and Taos, taking the high road from Nambé north, you will cross the mostly unmarked boundaries of four Indian Pueblos (Tesuque, Pojoaque, Picuris, Taos) and will add two more if you come back the main road (San Juan, Santa Clara, plus San Ildefonso off in the distance), which were "granted" to the tribes by the Spanish Crown or Mexican government—an early form of grandfathering. Plus the boundaries of all the other land grants, perhaps a half dozen in all, most of which were dismissed by the U.S. Court of Private Land Claims in the 1890s, although the land grants are still very real in the minds of many Hispanic residents of the mountain communities. Mostly unseeing, you will also drive over innumerable unmarked acequia channels, no two alike, each one half human shaped, half natural, each one embodying the quirks of generation after generation of diggers and irrigators, including two channels that irrigate my fields—if you detour down to Dixon. Then there are all those straight line boundaries, again mostly unmarked, between Forest Service and BLM lands, state sections, and private lands.

Since I am a member of the straight line tribe, a favorite pastime of mine is to parse out the remaining traces of the southernmost spur of the once-vast Denver and Rio Grande Western narrow gauge system, the Chile Line, which dropped down from Antonito, Colorado into New Mexico through Tres Ritos, Embudo, Española, San Ildefonso, and came up Alameda Street to Guadalupe in Santa Fe, to the brick station house that now houses Tomasita's Restaurant. Other salient relics include the circular stone foundation of the dual-gauge turntable, on whose site the Community Bank building now sits (an arc of brick wall denoting location and form of the turntable), the two redwood water towers at Embudo Station and Tres Ritos, Railroad Avenue in Española, and brown stubs of trestle pilings near San Ildefonso and elsewhere.

Traces of the roadbed can be detected from Rio Arriba County Road 582 just north of Española, up through San Juan and Lyden, along the west bank of the Rio Grande. Further north, from Velarde on, the old roadbed is clearly visible across the river from State Highway 68. At Embudo Station, reincarnated as a fashionable summertime restaurant, the rail line began its long ascent up the side of the canyon, La Barranca grade, once the site of a spectacular train wreck. Now a dirt track, a mile of it serves as a driveway for a half dozen houses.

Further north, on US 285, just out of Tres Ritos, the piñon-juniper woods recede and the sky takes over and the landscape opens up, rising mysteriously towards the immense mound of San Antonio Mountain, finally cresting at an undefined sagebrush lip that reveals the vast inland sea of the San Luis Valley. Through here the old Chile Line roadbed weaves back and forth, across arroyos and depressions, cutting through the clay and sand, snaking its way slowly up the rise. Every time I make that drive, once or twice a year, I struggle to keep my eyes on the mostly straight road while trying to remember where the old line has hidden itself, in what arroyo, behind what hill or outcropping of boulders, to right or to left now, until finally at the crest it reveals itself as a series of blurred cuts and fills marching off toward Antonito fifteen miles in the distance.

A few miles later comes the state line, indicated by the usual signs and a change in pavement material: straight, otherwise invisible, yet marking a change in philosophy, you might say, and a change in laws, the first of which you will notice is the speed limit.

Going north into Colorado, I think of the border as a line, a wall, a gateway. Returning south back into New Mexico, I begin to re-enter a circle, an enclosure, a place where some of the old lines, the less straight ones, the less cut and dried ones, the ones that are not the shortest distances between two points, still can guide the way, and I know I am coming back home.

|2000| The thing about an adobe floor is that it would be cheap. Cheap as in free.

Rose Mary and I had gone through the last of the one-time-only movie money from my first novel, converting it into two acres of land, construction supplies, and an old flat-bed Chevy to haul everything around. Financial swords into ploughshares. One-time-only because they never made the movie.

These were the good old days of free-for-the-asking dirt roofs, adobe bricks, mud plaster, and mud floors. All you had to own was the dirt, and not even all of that, because foraging for sand, rocks, clay was still permitted on BLM land, which our two acres adjoined at the bottom of the drive to the south, where the sand was, and above the acequia to the north, where the rocks and clay were.

So, the mud floor. The basic mix was the dirt from the future front yard, which had served well for our adobe bricks and for the dirt roof, and somewhat less well for the mud plaster, for our first two rooms, which we built June through October with the help of friends. I mixed the mud for the floor in a big old contractor's wheelbarrow, steered the heavy loads inside through the living room doorway, tipped up the handles and poured; and then Rose Mary spread, troweled, and smoothed the thick gooey mass over a base of white pumice (for insulation, free from the Pajarito Plateau near Los Alamos), on her hands and knees. Our small children, one and three, bundled up against the cold, pressed their noses against the milky plastic of the temporary windows or watched from the kitchen doorway. We worked from early morning until after dark, which we were able to do, still being young in early December 1971.

We made three mistakes. We poured the floor too thickly, we poured the thick floor too late in the season, and we got the mix wrong for the too-late, too-thick floor. It took forever to dry. In December we moved in on a carpeting of tar paper over the firm but still damp mud. When it finally did dry out, our winter housesitters, who had helped us make our adobe bricks, swept the floor so vigorously that the quarter-inch cracks became a network of fascinating little arroyos, which we bridged with thick hand-me-down throw rugs. Oh, pioneers.

In spring, we patched the worst areas with a sandier, less crack-prone mix, kneading it back into one piece, then sealed it with a liquid with the promising name of "floor hardener." The traditional binder was ox blood but there appeared to be no ready source of oxen anymore—and then there was the more delicate question of how, as then-vegetarians, we could justify the slaughter. The effect of all this—wavy walls, lumpy floors, rough-cut ceiling, rough-trimmed vigas—was to inspire some old friends on their first visit to our new house to ask, "How did you find this hundred-year-old adobe?"

Since then we have smoothed out much of the original roughness: professionally applied hard plaster on the walls in some of the rooms, some of the floors torn up and re-laid, and all the leaky, cold dirt roofs replaced with fiberglass insulation and metal roofing.

But the living room adobe floor remains a flawed, ancient presence. I say ancient not because it is all of thirty years old but because a kind of peculiar reversal has taken place. During construction, the house was surrounded by earth worn barren and compacted by footprints and tire tracks. Now, out the windows, you see only the acequia-fed lushness of orchard, flower bed, and lawn. The primordial barrenness of stone and dry earth is now inside, a rectangular slab the color of leather or chocolate, with the textural irregularities of stone, or skin, or parchment, or lichen, or crusts of bread, or of wood worn and resurfaced and patched and roughly burnished, or of cuneiform tablets. In late afternoon when the low slanting light picks out the irregularities, the mud floor becomes a monolithic presence suggesting that the room was built around it.

I have seen carefully and wisely laid adobe floors, which look little more interesting than concrete, lacking the geological quality of a history of corrected ineptitude. Our floor is a record of its accidents. You can make out where the original cracks once were, where they have been filled, and where potholes dug by the iron feet of our first cheap furniture have been patched with a slightly different mix, where new hairline cracks are opening up, places where the floor has been pitted and refilled.

We have repaired it a half dozen times, sometimes with clay brought back from road cuts above Abiquiu or most recently eastern New Mexico, although these deep reds all but disappear under the darkening effect of the linseed oil we occasionally seal the floor with. Last summer we completely emptied the living room and I patched all holes and cracks, using fingers to push the wet mud into cracks and a sponge for smoothing, then sanding it all down with a dry rag the next day. After a careful sweeping, Rose Mary brushed in linseed oil on hands and knees, sealing and darkening the powdery taupe-khaki surface, which we were able to re-inhabit in about a week.

There are times when I have fretted over the unevenness of the floor, but in repairing it again last summer I realized that under our wear and tear it will continue to evolve in ways that other surfaces within the house will not, surfaces that will be recovered, smoothed down, painted over, again and again. The history inscribed in the surface of our mud floor is a version of the history of the house we built with our own hands and of our lives in it since 1971. I re-read it often in tiny, granular episodes, during moments of rest, staring into space, daydreaming, and in those pauses between the major domestic events of the day. The white spot left by one of the three fledgling magpies we have raised. Pock marks and hairline cracks made by the heat in front of the fireplace. A rough arc, where we commonly move back and forth an old cottonwood log that serves as a footstool.

The floor is the closest I will ever get to owning a Dubuffet, my favorite painter, fellow student of the patina of surfaces underfoot. It reminds me of the days of baths in a tin tub on the kitchen floor of two-by-six wood mill ends, of years without running water, of all four of us and the dog sleeping in one room: it reminds me that this was the best we could afford. It has required a cash outlay of perhaps a dollar or two a year for linseed oil. And in its way, in the way of wear and patching and repatching, in its slowly evolving patina, the mud floor will continue to record the history of our steps and pacings, of things dropped and spilled and dragged.

A mud floor is perfectly sustainable, being infinitely repairable and finally recyclable. Some future owners of the house, our children or grandchildren, craving smoothness and regularity, may take a pickax to the earthen slab, and cart the four-inch-thick chunks outside—where I hope they will spread them out in the weather, letting the rain and snow soften them back into lumps of earth, exposing to light and moisture the tiny seeds hidden within, underfoot, all these years, seeds from which plants will grow again.

|1998| When you work on a small farm, you think a lot about boxes. You think about sizes, shapes, materials, stackability, cost. About waxed and unwaxed cardboard, wired wooden slats, pressboard ends, paper-covered slats. About depth, width, length, and the solidity of the bottom. You even develop a moral order of boxes, in which there are perfect boxes, good boxes, bad boxes, and totally useless boxes. There are active boxes, which go through endless cycles of being filled and emptied, and there are inactive boxes, which end up in a dark corner of the shed filled with some category of object you don't know whether to keep or throw away.

You become a collector of boxes. You scavenge them, you hoard them. You can weave a rich structure of resentment around someone who forgets to return a favored box you were foolish enough to lend. As you enter your shed or barn in the winter, you may wonder, "Where did all these boxes come from?" Or, at the other extreme, at the height of the season, "Where did all my boxes go?" When your boxes are all empty, you have too many. But when they are all full, you don't have enough.

I began farming with my wife, Rose Mary, in the early 1970s. We weren't sure whether our garden had got out of control or whether we had a small truck farm serving farmers' markets and a few restaurants in Santa Fe and Taos. In any case, we needed boxes.

Coincidentally, it was a time when solidly built wooden bushel boxes were being phased out by local apple growers in favor of lighter-weight baskets of wired slats for picking and dressy white corrugated-cardboard boxes for shipping.

We bought 150 of these old wooden boxes at a dollar apiece and less. I have heard them called palmer boxes. Many bore still-bright lithographed labels from the Yakima Valley in Washington, the Okanagan Lake region in British Columbia, and other fruit-producing areas of the Pacific Northwest: Blue Goose, Trout, Snow Owl, Golden Rod, Big Chief. In these intervening twenty-five years, all but a couple of those labels have faded away and slaked off.

The boxes were already of some antiquity when we acquired them. They were probably shipped into northern New Mexico with their cargo of apples in the 1950s or even the 1940s. Local fruit growers would have used them briefly once a year to pick and transport their apples up into Colorado or down into southern New Mexico and West Texas, tipping the fruit out into sacks or cardboard for roadside or door-to-door sales. Most of the year the boxes would remain stacked out of the weather in barns and sheds. They are so designed that two empty boxes, like opposing halves of a clam, can enclose a third. Most of the boxes we bought were in very good condition. Some had the names of their second-generation owners—many of them descendants of Spanish colonizers, proprietors of orchards of 10 or 20 acres at the most—stenciled or stamped or scrawled on the sides: Montoya, Roybal, Martínez.

Their eccentric-seeming dimensions probably record some aspect of box-making tied to ancient traditions of lumber sizing. And they were manufactured in the days when nobody thought twice about using 12-inch boards for boxes destined to be quickly thrown away—the days of seemingly inexhaustible Northwest old-growth timber. The ends, for example, are heavy $3/4$-inch pine stock, $12^1/4$ inches wide and $10^7/8$ inches high. Often these are of one piece, though more commonly they are of two or three pieces butted together with corrugated steel fasteners. The side panels are either of one piece, or else of two or three pieces fitted together with a shallow tongue-and-groove cut. The two or three bottom slats are stapled to the thick end panels and then further held in place by nailed-on cleats, which center the boxes on top of each other and reduce sliding on flat surfaces. As originally shipped full of apples, the boxes would have been closed with top slats as well.

Fully loaded, the boxes can weigh up to sixty pounds. You can stack them as high as you can reach. For the farmers' market at the peak of the summer, I load the pickup bed with a layer of boxes filled to the top with fresh onions, lettuce, arugula, spinach, beets, squash, and basil. Then on top of them I lay down two heavy plywood planks that serve for our counter at the market. On top of them I slide in another layer of boxes. On top of them I lay down various other planks that also serve for our display. On top of them go shallower trays of fruit, garlic and shallots, and bushel baskets of flowers.

Thus stacked, everything sits for the night, camper shell windows open for coolness, waiting for the fifty-mile drive at dawn to Santa Fe or Los Alamos. Once we arrive there and have unloaded the produce onto the countertops, the upended boxes serve as stands for the planks, hold paper and plastic sacks, and raise up the cashbox on the tailgate to a more convenient height.

In the old days when we were selling fresh produce to Santa Fe restaurants, we used to leave the boxes and pick them up at the next delivery—at least until kitchen staff people began filching them. Each year a box or two disintegrated beyond repair, with ends, sides, bottom all splitting at once. At first, when apple growers were still cleaning these boxes out of their barns, the losses seemed unimportant. Later, the boxes became rare. Now they are irreplaceable.

A few years ago I painted a half-dozen boxes a clear blue to help dress up the market stand. I coated quite a few others with linseed oil to slow their decay. The dry foothill climate of northern New Mexico is merciful to wood as long as it receives minimal protection of almost any kind. And every other year or so I put various young workers to renailing the boxes that had become wobbly with use—only to discover, at the height of the season, that these repairs often lacked the necessary sensitivity about rough edges, protruding nails, and other details.

Recently I began to look at my apple boxes through new eyes. I came to appreciate them as objects of unquestioned utility—even to treasure their simple elegance as manufactured objects of wood designed for the rough and tumble of daily use.

They have claimed a central role in the life of our little farm. They serve for picking, packing, storage, sorting, and even as temporary work stands in that sometimes shady, sometimes sunny area in the angle of our two garlic sheds. Rose Mary and I, and those who work for us, move them in and out of the sheds each workday, carry them down to the fields and back, and load them in and out of the pickups and tractor loader again and again over the course of the week, the month, the season, from May until November. In winter I stack them in the back of the shed out of the weather.

Our boxes are part of the way we walk, bend over, lift things. They are the source of most of the splinters we pull out of our fingers. They may even be the origin of many of the nails the tire-repairers have extracted from our tires over the years. They have become part of the basic character of the farm, an element of shared habits and gestures that make up a small node of the culture of work.

They are also the source of a farm taboo. All of our longtime farmworkers, including our grown children, know the first signs. A visitor arrives at the garlic shed. He sees an empty wooden apple box lying on the ground or standing upended at a convenient sitting height. He bends down and draws it near. And at least two of us, as if by a premeditated signal, will call out, "Please don't sit on the boxes." And a chair will be offered instead, or an upended plastic tub, or an old wire dairy crate.

Our visitor will no doubt think us a little mad, not knowing or caring that when you sit on the boxes and begin shifting your weight in the manner of sitting humans, you start springing all the nails. That is no way to treat a venerable farm friend of twenty-five years.

One August I finally became serious about repairing and painting my apple boxes. Perhaps it was the approach of old age—in myself. I had become again painfully aware of how much we all waste in material goods, in packaging, in clothing and vehicles, in all those things we discard hastily after too much neglect, objects that would be cared for and even highly valued in much of the poorer world, where they would be thrown away only after having been completely worn out.

In the past I did emergency repairs, just enough to keep a box operational for the season. But now I decided I would look a box over carefully and then do everything necessary to restore it to the best possible condition. All inevitably needed refastening, a matter of pulling out loose nails and re-nailing sides and bottoms with cement-coated nails—without splitting the still strong but brittle wood. Badly split sides, ends and bottoms could be backed or replaced with odds and ends from the scrap-wood pile, notably $1/4$-inch plywood left over from household projects and various bundles of flat molding picked up at flea markets. I soon discovered that there was no box too far gone to restore. I could repair ten or fifteen in a couple of hours in the afternoon—at a time when I was usually tired of field work.

But the real pleasure came in repainting them in bright blue and turquoise, which sealed the wood against the weather and acted as a kind of glue at the joints, and even reduced the risk of splinters. With the boxes dressed up in their new colors, we're motivated to take better care of them and make sure that none get left in the bushes at the end of a row down in the field or out in the weather all winter long.

With the help of these repairs, and with luck, the boxes could go another twenty years, maybe longer, perhaps almost forever. As I worked away through the August afternoons in the shade of a maple tree in the center of the drive, such thoughts gave me great comfort.

I was doing what I could to guarantee that my boxes at least might never be thrown away: a small victory in a massively wasteful world.

|2000| A desk, a chair, pens, pencils, a writing machine of one kind or another, and time, lots of time, more time than most people can stand to imagine, in some room or another: these are the writer's tools. Add place, less easy to define, the where you came from, the where you were exiled from, the where you would rather be, and what is just out the window.

Being a writer gives you license to go to a place just to be there, not to see the sights, not to investigate the politics, but to immerse yourself in language, landscape, weather, food, and whatever routines there may be just outside the door of the room in which you lose yourself in the images and memories you have brought along. Afterward, those rooms become the shorthand for those places.

My New Mexico writing rooms have been five. The first, a rented adobe in the Embudo Valley's Cañoncito, helped me finish my third novel, *Log of the S.S. The Mrs. Unguentine,* begun in a bare room on 38th Avenue and Geary, above a Japanese restauramt, in San Francisco. The next two rooms Rose Mary and I built ourselves, starting with our unfinished living room, where I perched on a stool and wrote on a high workbench for a winter, until we had built a round stone tower—more a pillbox—a hundred feet south of the house. The next winter revealed the tower to be too small, too cold, too dark, and too far from the house, and too close to the goats and the geese and the chickens and ducks and guinea hens. I couldn't emerge from the low door without a chorus of honkings and cacklings and bahs from my dependents, which in neurotic moments I would translate into "And how's the best-seller going?" Within a couple of years, I was back at a home-made

A WRITER'S ROOMS

16

desk behind the front door. I was in good company there. Jane Austen wrote her books behind her front door. Eventually, shyly, hesitantly, my first nonfiction book, *Mayordomo: Chronicle of an Acequia in Northern New Mexico*, emerged from that shadowy corner.

In the mid-seventies a journalist acquaintance offered me a small guest house just off Canyon Road for a month: simple furnishings, brick floors, windows out into a vague but infinitely suggestive landscape of barren branches and bright December sky. I wrote feverishly in the morning and scribbled notes for the next day's work in the afternoon, devouring Chekhov in the evenings. By the end of the month I had most of a first draft of my fourth novel, *Some Instructions to My Wife Concerning the Upkeep of the House and Marriage and to My Son and Daughter Concerning the Conduct of Their Childhood*.

Ten years later we began construction of our writing studios out back, on the strength of an NEA grant and a family mortgage, me downstairs surrounded by adobe walls, and Rose Mary upstairs with a splendid panorama of the valley, from the Sangre de Cristos to the east, and the dark basalt mesa above the Rio Grande to the west.

Other rooms elsewhere have given me nothing tangible yet I still remember the months spent in them with fondness: a reinforced concrete aparment whose courtyard looked down on the Pireaus yachting and fishing harbor then called Tourkolimano; a cold and graceless *chambre de bonne*, literally a garret, in the 16th *arrondissemont* of Paris, and then a loft, once a stables, on the rue du Cherche-Midi; a spacious living room of a house in the Dublin suburb of Killiney Hill, with a plate-glass window which looked out past incongruous palms to the Irish Sea; a small stone house at the bottom of an icy path at the MacDowell Colony, in Peterborough, New Hampshire, and then ten years later there a grander studio on the edge of a meadow.

And then were those places where I was able to gather ideas and images around me with such excitement and urgency that I remember those moments as the happiest of my life: an old stone house and courtyard in Molybos, on the Greek island of Lesbos, with its drafty rooms and sliver views of the Aegean; a third and top floor apartment (not long before used as an office by the film crew for *Zorba the Greek*) with a commanding view of the old harbor in Chania, on Crete, with its Sunday crowds of strollers and marching bands; an old noncommissioned officer's bungalow at Fort Worden, Port Townsend, which overlooked the Straits of Juan de Fuca, across from Seattle, and from which we took afternoon walks along the shingle shore and at night watched for deer and raccoons out the sliding glass doors; a cousin's sparsely furnished guest house in Seal Beach, just south of Long Beach, and the afternoon walks on the sand; and then a luxurious apartment at the Villa Serbelloni where, standing up from my desk, I could gaze down across manicured flower beds and olive groves to the town of Bellagio, on Lake Como.

These are the posts at which I have watched and waited. For those of us who are slow and reflective as writers, this is mainly what writing is about. I do most of my waiting, my writing, in my backyard studio. Deliberately I have chosen views more tantalizing than inspiring, views that will reflect me back into the room, not invite me outside: the unfinished north side of the house, a bit of the driveway, the mesa to the west, treetops through every window. The studio is where all my manuscripts, notebooks, and dictionaries have come to rest—and also now floppy disks, the old Olivetti Lettera 22 (which traveled around the world in more mobile days), and even my mother's Remington portable, on which I first learned how to type.

Yet there are times when this final nest seems too overbearing and cluttered to admit of new ideas, and that is when we throw notebooks and folding chairs into the camper and head for the further reaches of the primitive area of Heron Lake, near Chama. There Rose Mary will lose herself in her thoughts and her books, and I will spend the days sitting quietly by the lapping water, pen and pencil and notebooks at hand, slowing myself down to the point where I can begin to note how much life this seemingly quiet place actually teems with, both around me and then within me. How eventful in sky, in cloud, in breeze and wind, in flitting bird and rising trout, and the changing light from dawn to dusk, the empty days become out there.

This of course is the best writing room of all.

|1995| When the river lowers in July, exposing a skeleton of silt-covered stones in the shadows of the overhanging cotton-woods, I often walk back to the house from the swimming hole up the riverbed itself, rather than back along the road. In rubber sandals I splash through the shallow waters, cross-ing them twice from high bank to low bank and back again to reach the rock- and driftwood-strewn bank opposite the driveway. I am too practical to do this for the sheer pleasure of feeling the cool water wash over my feet and ankles in the heat of the afternoon, yet I know that such simple pleasures have their deeper uses.

I search instead for stones for future garden paths and walls and other domestic works. On each walk up I carry a flat stone, either one freshly pried out of the sand, or one I have discovered on an earlier walk and placed where I could easily spot it. They are a mix of blue-gray quartzite, mottled gray and red Embudo granite named for the northern New Mexico val-ley and the river itself, basalt, sandstone, and black shale, which a geologist friend would rather have me call phyllite—all from around nine to eighteen inches in diameter and three quarters of an inch to two inches or more thick. Anything much larger is too heavy for me to carry. I remember the younger man who once could do such things.

I find the best flat stones early on in the summer—large and thin, not all that heavy for their size. Soon, within a few weeks, I am reduced to toting smaller, thicker, and more domed pieces as the season advances, unless a good churning flash flood exposes a new crop. I have been doing this for three or four years only, to my regret, when I could have been doing it for twenty-five; but assuming that I will visit the river nearly daily I can count on an annual harvest of perhaps two hundred stones, enough to keep me busy with my occasional springtime rock works.

The river splashes down three steps that lie across its course at irregular intervals from a point opposite my driveway, down to the swimming hole one hundred and fifty yards downstream, to the west, in a slow S-curve, the steps being marked by bands of larger and more flood resistant rocks and boulders, around which are to be found the best flat stones. The smaller ones are distributed randomly here and there and require no great effort to find, especially the somewhat fragile pieces of black shale. By August, when I have well combed a two- to three-hundred yard stretch of the river between the gate and swimming hole and somewhat beyond both, I will tramp through the shallow water and tip underwater stones on edge to see if they are thin or flat enough for my purposes.

An excuse, in the end, to continue a childhood fascination with streams and shallow pools, or simply to prolong the afternoon minutes in the presence of rocks cleaned and polished by the clear water, along this winding path of stones over which lean the gray trunks and pale green leaves of an endless gallery of narrow-leaf cottonwoods. And there is something soothing, even healing, in staring at the myriad shapes, chaotic in some sense, of this jumble of rocks in all shades of color and every mix. Here is so much complexity that the mind can release its order-making grip and wander and speculate and dream and plunge.

Each one of these hard lumps has some incredibly long and complex history, which stretches back to the beginnings of time—yet a past of nothing more than geologic cataclysms between eons of relative immobility. "History" of course is not the right word, nor "time," nor anything else, for these objects that are as far as can be from our living substance—yet which, in infinitely powdered form, make up much of the fleshy, motile stuff of what we are. As I ply my way up the river each afternoon, as the clouds gather and the breezes drain down from the mountains whose shards and chips these rocks are, there is a question that nags at me just below those words floating, unloosened, inside my brain: "What is the kinship? What is the kinship between this warmth and quickness, and that hardness and stillness?" And coming like footfalls, the answer, which is no answer: "Everything, nothing, everything, nothing."

But once I bend down and move the stones and carry them away from the river and lay them out in the shade of the cottonwoods just inside the gate, then in some trivial sense they can be said to enter history, that human fencing off of a comfortable and almost comprehensible pen or garden within eternity, where mind and memory can play and know meaning and contentment, without fear, or with less fear, of evaporating into the vastness of it all.

I carry my flat stones into history: they will wait through the autumn and winter at the bottom of the drive, just inside the gate, until some spring day when I start up the tractor and drive down and scoop them up in the front end loader and carry them up to the house, where they'll add to the expanse of flat stones outside the front door we call the courtyard—it was once enclosed by a wooden fence—or outside the little stone tower that serves occasionally as a guest house, or to the steps that form a waterfall from a pipe coming out of the ditch bank. The stones will eventually become pathways leading from the studio to the house, the house to the tower or the driveway. There, underfoot every day, they will no longer trouble me with their insistent question. They will have become instead a record of ordinary gestures over the course of years and decades, the gestures of carrying stones from one place to another and re-setting them evenly, flatly, in the earth. They will have been assembled, as paths and courtyards, somewhat in the manner of thoughts and ideas themselves.

In the days when they were built of stone, and in the rocky places of the world, houses and villages, towns and cities, paths and roadways were the accretions of such gestures—land-bound coral reefs in large. Settling a place used to be largely a matter of rearranging the stones—or in the Southwest, of recasting earth itself into mud bricks and mortar, composed of the sedimentary remains of rock ground and pulverized into sand and clay.

The soils in which I farm were mostly rock in one form or another. Perhaps this accounts for the peculiar possessiveness I have about the rocks that surface in my fields, and also why I take pleasure in filling the front end loader with them and carting them back to my various rock piles near the gate, and along the dirt road that runs parallel to the river, piles overgrown with creeper and squawberry bush: I know that ultimately they will be useful, somehow.

The river grinds away, through all seasons, furiously in the spring, high in its bed, in a deep-throated roar, and quietly in the winter, sometimes so quietly that you must silence all thought to hear it. Each time the water passes over each stone, it makes a tiny noise. These lapping and tinkling sounds, conjoined with thousands of others, are the announcement of the first infinitesimal steps by which rock is converted to soil, upon which all embodiment will feed: life begins in a kind of music.

II WATER

|2000| I used not to visit the river much in winter. Early spring came before I took notice of it again, the water slowly rising and turning muddy and gathering speed and filling the banks, through late March and April and May.

Winter seemed a time of rest and retreat. The river became quiet, almost invisible, a thin ribbon of water made dark by shadow as it snaked its way through snow banks. On below-zero mornings it would flag its sunken presence with a curtain of mist and create short-lived traceries of frost on rocks and overhanging branches. I remained puzzled that it never froze solid across, accumulating only a fringe of ice along its banks even in the coldest winters—unlike the larger and faster Rio Grande a few miles below, at a point where an acequia weir gathers up chunks of ice formed in the shadows of the long gorge.

For many years I never climbed down the banks in winter to see what was going on. Perhaps I expected to find nothing. Or it was just enough colder down there, a few feet below the dirt road that runs along the river, in the shadows of the bare cottonwood branches, where even less sunlight filtered through. This would have been when I was still unused to cold and even afraid of it, before I had learned to regain a taste for the sharp dry air of northern New Mexico each winter, the hauntingly clear skies, and for the simplification such severity can bring.

Not long before reaching the valley, tributary trout streams gather together into one flow before stepping down from the high mountain valleys and tumbling through a rocky gorge, the Box, into the Embudo Valley. At this point it becomes known as the Rio Embudo. Ahead of it there lies a relatively sedate run of three or four miles before its final transformation, at the confluence with the Rio Grande.

A few years ago I started visiting the river almost daily in winter, at roughly its midpoint, on my late morning walks. I survey a segment somewhat less than a mile long, during which the river drops perhaps thirty feet in elevation through a series of runs and steps. Much of my walk is along the dirt road that parallels the river, but recently I extended it another quarter of a mile at an angle away from the road, along the river itself, along the inside of a wide bend, a small floodplain of boulders, sand, and willows and cottonwoods saplings working to reclaim it. There are two other places I often leave the road, push through brush, scramble up and down banks, to rejoin the water.

Magpies, flickers, ravens, dippers and mallards, me and the dogs, and the occasional stroller or runner are among the creatures conspicuously out and about during the day. The sky is subdued in movement. Infrequent storms slowly clot the sky, lower their darkening blankets, without the high-altitude fanfare of spring and summer thunderstorms. Most days the sky grows lighter and lighter into an intense blue and then deepens and darkens to star-studded black again, and the air remains still and breezeless.

In the windy bustle of spring and early summer it is easy to think of the river as just another feature of the landscape. Self-effacing, the water mirrors leafed-out trees and quick-changing skies, inviting you to look away and out and up at the cottonwoods and their silvery green leaves flicking in the light and wind, to the horizons of swelling treetops. The color and movement distract as the trees pump water and nutrients from the river up into explosions of color and fragrance. In the riot of growth it is easy to become confused about the deeper hierarchies. We take for granted the water. The river? But of course.

I can remember the shape of the cottonwood, the texture of the lump of basalt, the darting trout, or the call of the killdeer. But the river, that sly and elusive presence, flows wordlessly through my memory and then surprises me again when I return to its waters each day. When I bother to listen carefully, its movement always sounds different, perhaps as tuned by temperature, humidity, depth, speed, air pressure, and my own mood: sometimes soft, a flat washing sound as over gravel, and sometimes a hearty roar. When low, it issues distinct notes, musical. Higher, at a certain stage of flood, it hisses past. At full flood, six feet or more deep, boulders unloosen and bounce along the bottom with muffled bangs.

In winter, the river flows at stream speed, at a walking pace. There is nothing hurried about it. The water moves at the natural pace of most large ground creatures, a little faster than some, slower than others, at the pace within which we were created to view our surroundings, and to smell them, hear them, and touch them—before industrial civilization redesigned the world to be perceived at ten and twenty times that pace, from inside moving objects, through glass, through screens, with air and sound conditioned, with half our senses rendered useless.

The river slows me down in winter. I try not to jump in the car or truck at every excuse, to the point that driving comes to seem painfully noisy, an experience frustrating for what it first promises, yet immediately dismisses. Because of the press of some errand, to lose a day of walking among all those pebbles and rocks and trees and tangles of driftwood and stretches of fine gray sand, and the water: this becomes a painful deprivation. In winter I come to think of the valley, my fields, and my short stretch of river, and the bluffs overlooking all, as a world of unfathomable complexity that will occupy what is left of a lifetime in observation and reflection. There is something I do not know about that particular granite boulder, this New Mexico olive, the nuthatch, the mayfly. I must learn all these things. I will be lucky to learn a few. The details drop into place so rarely. There are so many. My curiosity is so slow. I have been blind and deaf to so many things for these decades. I need a thousand winters to master the knowledge of what lies beneath my feet.

Yet in my unseeing there may be more than just the solace of a short stretch of a small river, late in a quiet morning. There may be something else in this half-conscious banking up of images and sounds and smells, in the way they crowd out the insistent cultural images and noises of our time which urge us to be quick, thoughtless, and grasping. When I go each day on my walk and gather up these images of water, stone, and feather, twig and wood, and the sounds they make, and feel the gravel underfoot, I know I am a little safer. In their granular disorder, in their flow, in their thickets, they are the emanations of the power of a place studied and absorbed in daily habit; they are the grains and spores and seeds of a place, whose shapes give no hint of what ultimately may spring from them, in understanding.

In this winter mode, this river mode, of seeing the world, those cities given over to the automobiles seem barren and simple, patchily and thoughtlessly built to please none of the senses, only assault them. Yet I know that this is where most people live their lives, and at the pace of the city and the interstate highway and the jet airliner; and I know that much of the pain I experience in late spring comes from having to accelerate again, and learn how to thirst for speed and distance and the spectacular—if only to know how to talk to my fellows. The valley will then come to seem not the center of my universe but instead a small place you can drive through in a few minutes. The center will seem elsewhere, in the capitals of artifice, or wherever the electronic magic show of our age springs from, that anywhere else where I am not but always think I wish to be.

The river embodies the paradox. It determines so much of the nature of this small valley where I live. Yet it does not stay. It flows through, changing its waters every instant. So restless, yet so place-bound, while it walks continuously in and out of our lives, the noise of its presence, the noise of its vanishing. It is never the same river. You can never step in the same river twice. It is never here for long. Yet it is always present.

Winter is about water, the accumulations of snow and ice banked up and then released from the mountains, from the shadows of canyons and forests, in the warmer seasons. Snow and ice, such convenient storage arrangements. To springs and streams and rivers and oceans again, and then mist and cloud, and then to rain and snow and ice again.

Winter is about water, and about the river. It is the season that feeds the river in this slow and indirect yet clever way. Perhaps snow and ice came first. Perhaps they invented the river. The river is their solution, the link they created to form the cycle. Then the river invented the vegetation that lines its banks, and the fauna that inhabits its waters, to enliven its endless days and nights, including eventually the dogs and me, and all the other watchers and strollers.

This is what the river in winter tells me, as it wanders slowly past all who watch it, at a time when much other life has receded into dormancy and hibernation, alone or almost alone in its sound and movement, its waters slowly blackening and silting over the dead leaves in its depths.

The river is an inventor. I invented you all, it says as it rambles by, its waters disappearing around a bend beyond some overhanging willow branches, which marks the turnaround point of my walk.

I retrace my steps, returning home against the flow.

|2001| A couple of times each summer Rose Mary and I throw the cooler into the camper and fill up the water tank and head north for the shores of Heron Lake, a few miles southwest of Chama, in the very north of northern New Mexico. The arrival of August is a reminder that time is running out: the primitive campground, which we prefer, closes in mid-September, though not the regular campgrounds.

Invariably we stop at Bode's General Store in Abiquiu for provisions. Bode's is what a rural general store should be, stocked with the sort of hardware that will save the locals from a long drive to town to get that one essential thing, plus basic groceries with gourmet items that will appeal to campers seeking to compensate themselves in advance for the deprivations they are about to experience, and newspapers and gas. Our cooler filled to overflowing, the VW Westfalia gassed up, we head for the woods—munching potato chips all the way.

The drive is worth it just for the stunningly hued cliffs that ring the basin that encloses Abiquiu Lake and the Ghost Ranch, which give way to more subtle vistas on the remainder of the one-hour drive up through juniper-piñon forests and past the lush vegas of Tierra Amarilla and Los Ojos, with the cliffs of Los Brazos opening up to the northeast.

Los Vados and Heron Lakes are both reservoirs, not natural lakes, two of the more agreeable creations of the San Juan Diversion Project. Heron Lake, with its powerboat speed limit, is the lake for Quiet People. As a rule I consider reservoirs to be uninteresting bodies of water: edge zones between land and water are normally among the richest and most diverse habitats, but fluctuating water levels in reservoirs frustrate the creation of stable marshes. Yet I make something of an exception for Heron Lake—not named for its herons but for the San Juan Diversion visionary James Heron—owing to the tranquility of the site and its maze of inlets and peninsulas within the primitive campground and for the wildlife that is drawn to its shores, fluctuating as they are.

The primitive area is so named because once you pass the dumpsters and twin porta-potties at the entrance, you are on your own: what you carry in is exactly what you need to carry out. The often deeply rutted potholed track also indicates with slithering tire marks heading off into the bushes what happens when heavy rains hit. And last time we went, my cell phone announced that it was going camping too, thank you.

If we are lucky we'll score a favorite campsite at the end of one of those peninsulas with a view across the silvered waters to the distant Brazos Cliffs. Within a matter of minutes we'll have the camper parked in the shade of a ponderosa pine and the pop-top up and the propane refrigerator lit (though this can be hit and miss) and the camp chairs unfolded and table set up and we'll be paddling around in the warm top strata of sun-warmed water. Cares quickly sluice away.

I sometimes wonder why we go to the trouble. It amazes me how much food and water two people can go through in two days. And how much *stuff* we manage to bring along, both what is attached to the VW camper and what we throw into it. But much as I have always admired all those clever fold-up, light-weight, fits-into-a-little-pouch camping gadgets, I have never had the urge to pile any of that stuff on my back and head for the true primitive areas.

And maybe it's all relative. What we bring is paltry compared to the vast encumbrances of house, pets, fields, work, neighborhood, community, and endless restless activity that we leave behind for a few brief days. As a camper, even as a pampered car camper, I can sit outdoors and think and watch and swim and nibble all day long without having to worry about doing anything else at all, beyond those brief flurries of activity occasioned by meals and by going to bed and getting up in the morning. The simplest meals, framed by crisp dry mountain air and the scent of pine needles, become memorable gourmet events. The minimal clothing needed during the heat of the day serves as a reminder that one is a creature of the body, not of the wardrobe.

Hike? Explore? It's amazing how much exploring you can do sitting quietly in a chair all day beside a body of water, with a pair of field glasses within reach. You get to know what an unclocked day feels like again, a day of dawn and sunrise and ebbing shadow and noon and dusk and darkness, hour by hour, minute by minute, second by second, cloud by cloud, breeze by breeze, moments interwoven by the appearance and disappearance of birds, fish, deer, coyotes, insects, and at the end of the day the slow emergence of the planets and the moon and the stars and the occasional satellite—and once an effulgent weather balloon like some airborne jellyfish catching the last rays of sunlight high above, long after darkness had settled on us below. All to the calls and laughter and the slamming of doors and clattering of pots and pans of your fellow campers in the distance.

Two days of this kind of life probably refreshes more than a vacation of two weeks of negotiations with airports, airplanes, rental cars, and unfamiliar hotels. By the end of our stays at Heron Lake, I usually know who I am again, or who I should be, and am ready to re-enter the world centered again on the important things, often with a major decision thoroughly thought through.

Often but not always. Sometimes this is little more than the realization that we need to get back to Heron Lake far more often than we have in the past.

| 1998 | For thirty years, the acequia has been my teacher.

That experience began with the moment I stood on a wooden plank bridge and looked down into the slow-moving waters of the Acequia del Medio, in Dixon, in the Embudo Valley, as it flowed through the backyard of a crumbling adobe my wife and I were about to rent for $35 a month. I watched the water swirl down around an old apple tree and under a fence, into the backyard of a neighbor's place. The moment I saw this thing, whatever it was beyond a small channel of water, I knew I had found a home. That was late in the Indian Summer October of 1969.

With a certain brusqueness the acequia began to teach me about physical labor. It prodded Rose Mary and me to plant a garden just above its banks, the most laborious garden we have ever grown. It taught us to feed ourselves and therefore about that special form of health that comes from growing and harvesting and preparing and eating your own food. This was serious business now. Our son was a year old and our daughter was on her way. Our new neighbor, Henry Martínez, leaned over the fence each morning and patiently articulated those instructions the acequia considered too obvious to state itself.

The acequia gave me my first job in northern New Mexico, a job unpaid and thankless which yet abruptly connected me with thirty other families in El Bosque, on the other side of the river where we built our adobe house—and, because these were dry years, connected me to two dozen other comisionados and mayordomos running the eight other acequias of the valley.

The acequia is a strong teacher. Nothing else anywhere in

this country seems to be able to convince men young and old, and occa-sionally women, to labor together out there in the sun and rain and snow, sometimes day after day, for little money. Because this business of digging out a ditch together in these times seems so unbelievable—why would anyone want to do that?—it comes as a small miracle every year when a new crop of workers turns up bright and early on those mornings in March and April and May to do something as inelegant, unglorious, and undra-matic as dig out a ditch. For thirty years I have listened to people worry that next year nobody will turn up. But the acequia knows that despite our personal, individualistic doubts, parciantes and their workers will show up, because the acequia is giving them something they need and need very badly: a sense of community, a sense of engaging in labor essen-tial to themselves, to their neighbors, and their community.

More lessons, more lessons. The acequia insisted that I learn how to work with everybody in our community of prickly anarchists. Not just with the Martinezes, Gonzaleses, Valdezes, Archuletas, Atencios, and my hippie Ph.D neighbors, but everybody—especially, it sometimes seemed, those who drank too much or smoked too much or who were angry at everything and everybody, especially me. The acequia patiently explained to me why feuds develop in small places but it also suggested how people could make up their differences, and why they had to, at least now and then, at least once a day, or at least on those days when they needed to irrigate.

Consensus? Mediation? Conflict resolution? I got a quick lesson in all that at the Cañoncito turnoff in the heat of July and August after-noons where the comisionados from the three Lower Ditches assembled for their self-righteous vigilante runs up to the four Upper Ditches to take what was rightfully theirs—though the acequia made us tone down our rhetoric and become almost polite by the time we got to the house of the first Upper Ditch commissioner.

You see, the acequia explained, what dry years are good for is to make people work together again and cooperate and realize how interde-pendent they all are. Therefore, the acequia subtly suggested, the most abundant times, the most materially prosperous of times might not be the best times for people and their communities.

The acequia taught that it doesn't care at all about your last name or the color of your skin or how long you have lived anywhere, though it did suggest that settling down in one place and sticking with it would best serve its ends. It has mapped its progress across multiple cultures through its lexicon of terms in Arabic, Latin, Spanish and now English. In this, the acequia is like the ancient Greek institution that now finds itself the object of aspiration in virtually every society in the world: democracy.

Eventually the acequia taught me how to farm and to make a living from our fields. It had a real interest here. Acequias cannot be kept alive simply because they are venerable institutions or by being turned into charming scenic cultural antiques; they can remain alive only if they are used, only if the labor and care that has gone into their creation and which continues to go into their upkeep and maintenance, only if this collective communal labor is echoed and honored and supported by an ongoing, equivalent labor in the fields that the acequia's channel feeds with water year after year.

The acequia prods us to remember that we can grow healthier, obviously fresher and tastier food in our fields and backyard gardens than we can get anywhere else, and that if we use our own labor to do so and the labor of our friends and neighbors, we are far more efficient in energy terms than the largest agribusiness farms in the world. The acequia whispers that we can revitalize our communities by doing so. It knows that in a world which each day invents yet another noose of corporate dependency, in a world constructing a labyrinth of dependencies on nonrenewable fuels, it knows that the one last act of true independence by humankind may lie in the simple ability to plant a seed and open a ditch gate—until at least our seeds are finally taken away from us, licensed away, patented away, bio-engineered out of our hands.

Farming, like acequia work, is where culture and nature negotiate with each other. By drawing me into my fields, and up and down its banks, and to its source, which is the river, the acequia lured me into the natural world—not as a spectator, not as a recreationalist, but as a fellow worker, as a steward. I cannot list all the details the acequia has revealed, nor how much I have learned of the myriad other creatures with which we share our water, our air, our earth. The acequia has been my guide. Certain places along the acequia I have been privileged to know—a bend shaded by cottonwoods and junipers, a weathered wooden flume sluicing the water across an arroyo—are among the most beautiful places on earth.

In this arid climate, the acequia has a clever idea. It diverts water from the river in order not just to spread it over the land of our fields but also to create countless habitat corridors out into the fringes of our river valleys, right into our backyards, and it will charge and recharge the aquifers beneath our feet—thus helping our rivers, which we tend to regard as dumb, irresponsible beasts, temper their flooding ways and in turn help us through periods of drought. Amazingly it does all this without pumps. Gravity is quite enough for it. The acequia, I suspect, is shocked that anybody might consider this a somehow wasteful arrangement. Leaks are what the acequia is all about.

Tens of thousands of other people have learned these things and more from the acequia on this continent and others, over the past several thousand years. For anyone pondering the future of northern New Mexico, I would suggest that the acequia must be central to deliberations, not peripheral.

As it will be the first to remind us, the acequia is not just about water: it is about who we are, who we wish to be, and how we as a species relate to a natural world that is each day pointing out the consequences of our past mistakes.

|1990| Everyone has been startled at least once by the miraculous imagery of the saying that water can be made to flow uphill toward money. It is the genius of the image that it seems to settle for a moment the arguments that bring it into play. Everything has its price. We live in a world of buying and selling. What else can we say?

Yet we also live in a world of other kinds of value, and sooner or later we will need to ask whether it is good for anything but money for water to be made to flow uphill, and whether it is bad for streams, rivers, traditions, communities, and even individuals.

Some time ago I sat in on a water rights adjudication hearing in Santa Fe—my first, so I was able to pretend to view it through somewhat innocent eyes. There was the small, cramped courtroom in the old stone Federal Courthouse, probably not unlike courtrooms and hearing rooms where these proceedings have droned on in New Mexico for hours and days and months and even years and decades. There were the twenty-five or thirty silent, patient defendants from the far north village of Questa, who were landowners, working men, probably miners or former miners, Hispanic all, dressed in plaid western shirts and cowboy boots. There were the attorneys and legal assistants for the New Mexico State Engineer Office, four in all, Anglos all, with their table covered with huge aerial photographs, yellow legal pads, clipboards of lists, notebooks. There was the defendants' table, presided over by a lone attorney from Northern New Mexico Legal Services and a volunteer assistant from Questa. There was a tripod from which hung detailed maps of the section of Questa being debated, with parcels of land blocked out in green and red and pink. There was the imitation wood paneled box of the witness stand where sat, during my time there, a succession of Mr. Raels and Mr. Valdezes. There was the judge, a kindly black-suited gentleman who patiently elicited and presided over a river of minutiae about fences and culverts and walls and houses and ditches and pastures and the placement of this or that boulder, all of which made up the substance of the proceedings.

What I witnessed for a few hours was the operation of that legal mechanism by which water is prepared for its eventual pumping toward money. It has to have its claims of ownership documented, it has to have its title quieted, it has to be made merchantable, salable, which is what enables it to be freed up from land, acequia, community, and tradition. A horrendously expensive process in itself, this elaborate preparation, as anyone can easily estimate by calculating the legal hours, the research time, surveying time, driving time, lost work hours for the landowner defendants, and so on, that must go into a hearing of this sort, which in this case lasted well over a week. And this was a minor one at that, concerning some relatively small parcels of land that had been left out of a previous adjudication suit. And in the larger sense there may never even be an end result. The number of re-adjudication suits being opened up suggests that the process may well be perpetual. And who pays? In a state with a regressive tax structure, the expense of it all will be disproportionately born by those most likely to suffer from its effects. And wherever there has been an end result, it has been to pave the way toward the dissolution of the traditional connection between land and water, and to break down the fragile webbing that binds water to land and to acequia and to what may be called community itself in the rural areas of northern New Mexico. In short, the adjudication of water rights is social policy disguised as something else.

Yet there was something dully reassuring about the hearing. No sparrow that fell thirty years before would be overlooked by the court, no garden grown by a grandmother or tenant or neighbor or friend, within living memory. But before my eyes began to glaze over and my own memory set about sorting through other lists, the grand oddness of it all flashed through my mind. There was something missing. Questa was here, in this courtroom, but also most obviously, in the deepest sense,

Questa was still where it was, spread out over the sloping land a hundred or so miles to the north, in the shadow of the northernmost peaks of the Sangre de Cristo Range in New Mexico. What we were looking at was a Questa that had been evaporated out of its real setting to be reconstituted here, in distilled form, on paper, in words spoken in the courtroom—a Questa which had been driven through the abstract filters of quantification and the law, depositing a powdery residue of its real self in the courtroom. The proper place for these hearings, I thought, should be in the very fields and orchards and gardens of the actual landscape, and they should be conducted while climbing fences, wandering down driveways, walking ditches, sitting on boulders, while eating and drinking, in the bright sun or the wind and the rain and snow—not here, under fluorescent lights, in air that has been warmed too many times by the city's fevered lungs.

Water should go—we all know—to those who tend it, who use it, who love it, who dance for it, and it should flow downhill from stream to river, and river to sea. Yet we have licensed our society to scheme for it to flow toward those with power and money, and we have turned over our public servants to them, we have in effect given them the keys to the treasury so that no expense will be spared in drawing lines, making maps, conducting research, surveying boundaries, and filling vaults and basements with mountains of legal testimony.

What is oddest of all—I thought as I regained an open sky fretful with the sharp winds of a March afternoon—is that this legalistic hair-splitting over water rights needs the long-term ratification of the weather in order to work at all. And the weather, of course, is what no one can ever bring to court. Being, I suppose you would say, above the law. Capable, in short, of rendering the vast social labor of adjudication quite irrelevant—in these times of rapid climate change all over the globe. A kind of higher adjudication of the environment, you might say, that could be trying to tell us that fooling around with the elements is something we should think and talk long and carefully about before anything else, and in ways that make us all more neighborly, not less so.

| 1989 | I've just walked into the restaurant.

It's noon, Wednesday, August 23rd, 1989. The place is full. I should be fifty miles north of here at home working, not here, not now, anyway. I know about half the people in the dining room—fellow farmers and gardeners from Santa Fe, Chimayó, Española, Ojo Caliente, Embudo, Dixon, plus farmers' market board members and county agricultural extension agents and restaurateurs. The room is one of those places you enter at an angle to, at a corner of the parallelogram or trapezoid or other odd shape that makes up the floorplan. Everything runs at angles, as perhaps in nature. A low wall slices right across the middle of the room, making for a peek-aboo effect.

Only an hour and a half ago I was changing out of sopping holey shorts and a work shirt stained with tractor grease. I got my onions picked and washed and boxed up. Tomorrow's the Los Alamos Farmers' Market, and I had to get a few things done before I climbed into the pickup to make the fifty-mile drive down here to Santa Fe for one of those special events that always comes at the wrong time of day or the wrong day of the week or the wrong month of the year or all three. This is one of the latter. But here I am. Where do I sit? Who do I sit with?

Directly in my flight path a couple I know beckons me towards a landing. They are the Hammetts, Kingsley and Jerilou. They are editors and publishers of a local business newsletter that has a penchant for taking up lost causes and which likes to point out where things like the social safety nets are coming unraveled.[1] I sit down. A neighboring farmer is also at the table, an apple grower downriver from my place, Harvey Frauenglass, who makes what a lot of people think is the best organic apple cider sold at the Santa Fe Farmers' Market. He and I share a common institution in our pasts, the University of Chicago, which has marked us both as permanent idealists who have to live in a world far different from the one we were prepared for—if we were prepared to live in any real world at all. Probably not. We've talked of forming a University of Chicago Alternative Alumni club to help educate the public about the fact that universities like Chicago turn out low-income apple growers and garlic farmers too, not just Nobel Prize physicists and chemists and economists. Both of us are writers, too, another curse.[2]

All of us are here for that supposedly mythical offering, the Free Lunch. The host restaurant is Rick Post's Pranzo Italian Grill on Montezuma Street. The pink sunset atmosphere and indirect lighting of the place tells us that this is the height of fashion. Nice atmosphere, good healthy buzz of the conversations of thirty full tables of people who mostly know each other and who are getting to know each other better. Pranzo's, or the Pranzo, as I really ought to call it, is the latest business to open up in the refurbished Sanbusco[3] Center at the edge of the old railway yards near downtown Santa Fe, in the Guadalupe Street area, a yuppie belt that has sprung up in response to the seizure of the old downtown Plaza by the forces of aggressive tourism. About the only real business left on the Plaza is the old Woolworth's but from a certain kitschy point of view even that can look like a tourist trap.[4]

At each place setting there is a typed list on the Pranzo four-color letterhead describing the five courses of the free lunch, each course prepared by a separate restaurant from ingredients supplied for the most part by the farmers in attendance. Were I not a chicken-sandwich-for-lunch man, I would find it all mouthwatering. Instead I look on it as sociology.

"What is *smokey Chipotle?*" someone asks.

"I don't know," somebody else says.

Kingsley Hammett leans over the table and loudly confides in his raspy voice, "I hate these events."

I agree out of politeness. I haven't been to enough free lunches to know whether to hate them, love them, or be indifferent to them. My first encounter with the Hammetts came over the phone. They are a strikingly handsome couple. Kingsley: tall, athletic, the sort of fellow you expect to suddenly dash away in pursuit of a soccer ball. Jerilou: shapely, dark, sleek, shorter by a head, comes on tough but will finish an exchange with a winning smile and a just-checking shrug. She was the one who first called a year ago to complain to me insistently and articulately about plans for moving the Santa Fe Farmers' Market out of a senior citizens' center parking lot down in the barrio on Alto Street up into the newly refurbished Sanbusco Center parking lot, which is closer to where people go for other things and which is more visible besides. As Farmers' Market board chair I had to listen courteously and patiently to her many good arguments. I was stunned by her methodical attack and a quarter of an hour later hung up the phone convinced that I had made a lifelong enemy. The market made the move nonetheless. It's been a success for the farmers though, true, it hasn't done any good for the Alto Street barrio we left behind, nor for the public housing projects with easy walking distance of the old site.

I met the Hammetts later that summer in the Sanbusco parking lot where they became regular Saturday customers at the market. I don't think that meant that I won the argument. I was and still am chairman of the market board of directors[5] and very much favored the move because the Sanbusco management wanted us there on their parking lot every Saturday and Tuesday morning, while it was never that clear that the City of Santa Fe really had much use for us down on Alto Street. Getting the key to the john was always a big deal. Finding somebody to talk to about getting a key to the john was another big deal, among other things. And Joe Schepps, who turned the old warehouse buildings that used to house the Santa Fe Builders Supply into the present complex of shops and offices and eateries, even came to one of our board meetings in Española. We welcomed him as a hero—for driving twenty miles north to that much maligned town—and he loved every moment of meeting with our feisty farmer board, even agreed to take care of our insurance, which was tending to eat up most of our $3,000 annual budget. In exchange we give him and his tenants visibility by attracting a couple of thousand people to his parking lot twice a week. The only better place I can think of for the market is the downtown Plaza itself, which is where it should have been put a long time ago.

My wife Rose Mary and I started selling produce at the Farmers' Market in the early 1970s, somehow managing to pilot a succession of elderly Chevy trucks (1947, 1953) laden with lettuce and carrots and beets and turnips and onions and squash down the fifty-mile two-lane highway without mishap or breakdown for a couple of years. Then we moved on to other outlets. But I started going back to sell at the Farmers' Market around 1984 when I began to consider that maybe the Farmers' Market was one of those modest institutions that was having a sustaining effect on small-scale farming in northern New Mexico, an institution, if you can call it that, that wasn't one of those do-good projects or programs that inevitably topple over from the weight of their own overhead. It was and is just simply a place to sell whatever you can grow twice a week from June until November. And maybe I was hankering after something I knew I might never experience again, those weekly fruit and vegetable markets along the Boulevard Raspail in Paris, when I was continuing my career in idealism at the Sorbonne in the late 1950s.

Anyway, somewhere along the line, some Saturday morning at the market, at the tailgate of our '73 Dodge pickup, the Hammetts and I got into a conversation on how I thought they should do a piece on water use in northern New Mexico, in their business newsletter. "Great," they said, "we'll do it." I told them that one of these days we'd get together somewhere else than at the market, where I have to maintain three conversations at a time after having been up since a quarter to five AM; we'd find some quiet place where I could put my thoughts together out loud for their article. I'd thought about writing one myself, something different from the book I'd written about my experiences as mayordomo or ditch boss. A couple of years had elapsed since then, since the writing, not the publication[6], and I probably had a wider view of what was going on. But I had never got around to it and wondered whether I ever would.

So here we are at Pranzo's at noon, for our free lunch, at a time when we all really need to be somewhere else except in a fancy restaurant like this where we're trying to be gracious and pretend that we have lots of time on our hands. I was out in the field at 7:30 this morning pulling my Walla Walla sweet onions and dumping them into the tractor loader while waiting for my daughter Kate and Kiva Duckworth, a childhood friend of hers who works for us, to drive the pickup over from the house to begin picking what I estimated would be twenty-five bushel baskets of statice flowers in yellow, white, dark blue, light blue, peach, and pink. The weather has at last turned hot and dry enough to bring the blooms into full efflorescence. I helped the young women until 10, then ran the tractor home and hosed the dirt off the fat yellow onion bulbs and their green tops and boxed them up until about 10:30, then dashed inside to shower off the sweet scent of the onions, then climbed into the Mazda diesel pickup and headed for Santa Fe, hoping I wouldn't be too wiped out from the hundred-mile round trip and the free lunch to resume picking four or five bushels of basil after dinner and to pack the truck at dark for the Los Alamos Farmers' Market, which I set out for at 5:25 or 5:30 the next morning, also in the dark.

But I'm supposed to be here as part of the event. The Santa Fe Farmers' Market is a co-sponsor of it. I'm supposed to say a few words afterward as an aid to digestion. I have prepared a page on the connection between what we will have eaten and the working landscapes of the villages and valleys of Northern New Mexico. The event is called "A Taste of Summer Produce," a miniature version of a similar event that takes place in the Bay Area. The idea is to get farmers and buyers from restaurants together over a lunch cooked up out of produce grown in northern New Mexico. The five restaurants doing the cooking are picking up the tab for the lunch, which follows a sort of mini trade show of farmers displaying their wares to potential buyers out in the old Sanbusco lumber racks. Nice idea, but I've tended to look on it as an imposition on my picking schedule. One of the things we did in the mid 1970s, Rose Mary and I, was to sell exclusively to Santa Fe restaurants for a couple of years. I can tell you all about selling to restaurants. But true, things have changed, and now the tourist season more nearly matches the growing season, and perhaps a few restaurateurs in town have redesigned their kitchens to make room for the added mess which cleaning and processing fresh fruits and vegetables causes in comparison with neatly and compactly packed canned and frozen produce. And I did get my onions picked and packed in time, I made it down, and here I am sitting at a table with the Hammetts and Harvey.

"I hate these events," says Kingsley, as I said.

"I do too," I politely agree, though I think I might be beginning to enjoy being here after all, where I'm sitting in a soft chair, not squatting, stooping, standing, scurrying, not carrying heavy boxes of produce.

Then it occurs to me that maybe this is the time the Hammetts and I should be having our little chat about water so they can finally get that piece written for their newsletter. Here we are all sitting around the same table trying to think up chitchat subjects. So I put it to them.

Kingsley and Jerilou look at each other. "Sure," they say, "why not?" Harvey nods his assent.

I do realize, let it be known, that my suggestion is boorish. What I'm proposing to do is to monopolize the conversation through the next five courses. This is perhaps slightly less boorish than simply going ahead and monopolizing the conversation without asking permission first.

So I begin. I'm into my third or fourth convoluted sentence when Jerilou reaches over and touches my wrist. "Wait a minute," she says, pursing her full lips. She turns to her husband. "Kingsley, I think we should tape this."

"Tape recorder's in the car," he says, getting up with a flash of linen napkin. "I'll get it."

So I park myself back in the limbo of those awaiting the arrival of the media apparatus, which Kingsley shortly carries in, finds to be non-functional, makes functional, tests. It's one of those miniature cassette recorders you use to take down the proceedings of board meetings and such.

"Okay," says Jerilou.

Rewound, I rebroadcast a new version of my four sentences. The noise level in here is high but at least I'll be warming myself up for my after-lunch remarks, when I'll have to shout even louder. Water. I'm talking about water, about how it's been managed for hundreds of years in the countless small villages tucked into valleys and on the floodplains of the Sangre de Cristo Range, the southernmost spur of the Rockies. A waitress is about to pour an Italian white wine into my glass. I raise a hand. "Only a drop or two," I say, "a taste. I have picking to do later."

Not that she'll have any idea of what I'm talking about, it instanta-neously occurs to me. Begin to explain something and you end up hav-ing to explain everything. But she has moved on.

I continue: "There exists, there is already in place a rural infrastruc-ture of community in northern new Mexico that has miraculously survived all kinds of mistreatment by the powers that be over the past several hundred years. Being of course the one thousand acequias, the one thousand community irrigation ditches whose water courses wind through every village and town and which are still active and functional. Only one thing. They oddly don't know their powers, they don't act in the manner in which they have been empowered to act, as bodies politic, as subdivisions of the state of New Mexico on a par with municipalities and counties."

Jerilou is looking across the table at me with the studied patience of one who is wondering to herself, *What have we got ourselves into, what is this man talking about?*

But I should make something clear. These are not my exact words. I've had this conversation a half dozen times, a dozen times over the years, in whole and in part, to myself and with others. In re-creating my words at the free lunch I am saying what I would be saying if I were to say it over, now, at that table, at Pranzo's.

The waitress is back. She sets down a platter in the middle of the table. We all stare. We all pick up our menu sheets. We read:

NEW MEXICO ANTIPASTO
Chilled Barbequed Eggplant, Two Bean Ratatouille,
Roma Tomato slices with Goat Cheese and Opal Basil,
Tear-drop and Cherry Tomato Salsa
PRANZO ITALIAN GRILL

The platter is passed around. We shovel portions of each onto our plates. The little appetizer things are so artfully arranged that you could wonder whether magnifying glasses and tweezers were employed. Usually I eat too fast and gobble everything up, to the consternation of my table mates better schooled in how many times to chew their mouth-fuls. The virtue for one like me in monopolizing the conversation is that

I must fit my mouthfuls into the pauses between thoughts, into those moments when the contradictions in any set of ideas suddenly and embarrassingly reveal themselves, those moments when that keystone concept which is supposed to drop into place suddenly decides to arrive late or even get lost on the way.

"But why is all of this important?" Jerilou wants to know, looking up from her plate. From previous conversations and debates I know that this could be a feint, to lure me into a rhetorical ambush.

Why? "The ditches, the acequias, are what have held the landscapes of northern New Mexico in place for generations. This very landscape is now a considerable tourist asset—excuse my terminology—but it is also about to be dismantled—or rather, over-run by suburban sprawl and whatever you call the proliferation of mobile homes and mobile home parks. The ditches are a way to save the valleys and the villages. In effect you give them the power they already possess."

"What power?" Jerilou asks. "And also really why? I mean, *why?*"

I ignore the "why." In the way you tend to ignore the question that suggests that the people you have been confiding your innermost thoughts to perhaps don't share the same values after all. Don't we all know why? Or do we? I thought I just explained that.

I file that one for later. Jerilou and Kingsley are journalists. Their business is to ask questions and to keep asking them until they get the answer they want. I'll have to think about it. In the meantime, I'll stick to the how, which is always easier. To the power the ditches already possess. If you're new to this problem, all you need to know is that irrigation ditches or acequias that carry water to countless gardens and pastures and farms are governed by three commissioners who take care of the paperwork and a mayordomo or ditch boss who moves the actual water around, and that commissioners and sometimes the mayordomo are elected by their own neighbors, the landowner water users. But every ditch is a little different, so there are probably countless variations on the basic scheme.

Slow-motion, the delicate leaves and slices disappear into mouths. I go on: "What is needed is to support and reinforce something that is already there. The only kind of assistance acequias get is long-term credit for capital improvements like diversion dams and headgates, plus the engineering designs for such structures, which the Soil Conservation Service works up. Anything else, forget it. And then, too, when a ditch gets loans and grants to make capital improvements, we have to use Soil Conservation Service engineers. We can go shopping for a contractor, take bids and all that, but not for the design of the actual work. And in my experience, their engineers, sorry to say, are not the best. On our ditch we had a small project for a desagüe, a turnout or sluice gate, that was going to come in at about fifteen hundred dollars. The idea was that we wanted to be able to turn off the ditch where it goes under the highway, an easily accessible location in a flood or other emergency situation, unlike our diversion dam which is another mile up the valley and which takes a walk down through a long and often muddy orchard to get to. Some of the best emergencies happen at night, in the dark. Anyway, the Soil Conservation Service calls us up and says that because of some budgetary deadline not of our making we have a day, one day, twenty-four hours to make up our minds on the desagüe design, which doesn't look like it has a pipe big enough to take the whole ditch, which it would need in order to shut it off at that point. We have to take it or leave it, period. No time to modify the design to fit our needs. We take it. It is built as designed. And of course it doesn't do what we want it to do, completely shut down the ditch by throwing all the water back to the river. I'm no engineer, but I've had twenty years of handling water, our water, and I'm probably more of an expert on the habits or our particular stretch of river than any engineer. And I'm not exceptional in this. Thousands of commissioners, mayordomos, farmers and ranchers have been watching rivers and streams for generations, and my feeling is that the engineers listen to them only when they have to."

I pause for some chewing and tasting. Everybody is eating with the shifty-eyed look of those attempting to keep track of two things at once. I worry fleetingly about Harvey, though then realize he became involved with the acequia that runs fetchingly under his hillside front porch as soon as he and his artist wife bought an old adobe and large apple orchard about four miles down river from our place. He's about eight years older than I am but with our graying, grizzled looks and deliberate manner of talking we are often mistaken for each other.

"Then there are other problems. For example, short-term credit. No bank will lend a ditch money unless a commissioner goes in and personally co-signs the note, which I have had to do. Imagine running a business of any kind, or a city or a county government, without credit. Then there's the question of what I would call technical support, of how to keep records, run meetings, basic stuff that a lot of ditches could use some help with. There's no one to do it. Nobody trusts the State Engineer because we all know they're out to get us in the long run."

"Wait a minute," Jerilou insists with lowered voice and frown. "What does the State Engineer have to do with it?"

I've been aware of shoveling some delicate morsels into my mouth and grinding them up with my teeth, swallowing. The little slice of tomato with goat cheese and a leaf of opal basil went by too fast. For this kind of eating you need a soundproof room where you can nibble away at things with your incisors up front, metering bits across your taste buds in controlled doses, without fear of distraction.

"I'm getting to that. After I make the point of how big this thing is." Maybe. The thing being the arcane, legalistic, labyrinthine subject of the adjudication of water rights. I advise myself to hold my tongue. "Look, in the northern counties you've got a thousand ditches run by elected volunteer commissioners, three per ditch, plus a usually paid mayordomo, one per ditch, a usually modestly paid mayordomo, plus sometimes an assistant, you've got some four thousand volunteers working away in the villages keeping the ditches running, including Harvey here."

"I'll say," Harvey groans in assent.

"They need a bit of recognition. Volunteer firemen who serve for twenty years receive a modest retirement check every month. Their labors keep my house insurance low. Likewise, the labor of commissioners and mayordomos conveying water to what would otherwise be dry land do a great deal to hold and even increase property values. Imagine having our roads and highways repaired and maintained by volunteers or for that matter our power lines, gas lines, phone lines. For some reason we are not taking the management of our watercourses as seriously as our other utilities."

I may be being a little self-serving here. I've been mayordomo for going on five years and was commissioner for twelve years before that. I'm fifty-two. Rose Mary keeps asking me what kind of retirement we'll get. Social Security, I tell her. How much is that? she has asked. You don't want to know, I've told her.

I lunge on. "You could start by just making people conscious at first of how many ditches there are and where they run by putting up signs every time an acequia flows under a roadway. Ditches are mostly invisible to outsiders. I know the names of the nine or so ditches in my valley but not anywhere else. Putting all those names on signs, like we do for rivers and towns and county lines and such, would bring into circulation a whole wonderful pool of Spanish names that are not in currency outside of each little community. Like the wonderful rambling name of Harvey's ditch."

Harvey raises a hand indicating he needs to swallow first, then intones: "La Acequia de la Junta y Cienega."

"That's all very nice," says Jerilou, "but there's something I still don't understand."

I look across our empty plates at her. She's staring at me. So's Kingsley. Which point have I failed to make? When you're trying to explain something so close to you that it's inside you hidden away somewhere and you know you can't quite get at it even though you know it's all there somewhere, it was all there the last time you looked, in desperation you make a bowl-shaped gesture as if hoping the missing pieces will flow up into it or drop into from high, which is what I do. Struggling to say that this matter is of such urgency to me and probably to Harvey as well and why it should be of equal urgency to Kingsley and Jerilou Hammett or anyone else, why in some deep sense it's a matter of life and death to a place you love. But there. There it is. Why indeed is it a matter of life and death?

I realize I have failed to answer the question of Why save the acequias, Why save the traditional agrarian landscape of northern New Mexico.

"Look," I go on, "there's something unique in these communities, in the acequias, that corresponds to nothing in my own Anglo background, except perhaps for the New England town meeting. The water the ditches convey to the gardens and orchards and fields is not important anymore in the way it used to be, people can survive without it, yet it is also of supreme importance, as I have learned again this summer. We've just been through the worst dry spell in years. The urgency with which my neighbors demanded their share of water told me how important it still is to them. They told me at all hours of the day and night. Some of them stayed up all night to water their gardens. Some of them lied for their water."

"But people do that even when it's not a matter of life and death. That's people," Jerilou observes.

True. But inwardly I protest. Rose Mary and I farm. We farm in beautiful surroundings. We have something to do with the way things look around the fields we work. I grow onions and garlic because of some psychic deal made somewhere between me and the alliums, an arrangement founded on—what?—a kind of mutual respect—though the words are too awkward for the subtle realities that entwine crop and grower. We grow flowers for color and brightness, and they pay the bills better than the other things we also grow. I grow basil for the scent that can massage even my fossil-fuel-abused sense of smell. I do the tractor work, picking, planting, weeding, building, and the accounts, and while Rose Mary helps in all these things, she mainly turns the flowers and garlic into finished arrangements and tends the shop we share with La Chiripada Winery and Pottery in Taos and keeps the house going.

The Hammetts know this, or some of it. I can't remember whether they've ever come to the farm, whether they've ever turned off the highway and followed the wooded lane down along the river, a quarter of a mile to our place in Dixon. In the summer I spend my working day in the field in front of the house or up the road on the three acres we rent from a neighbor or across the river on another couple of acres we own on the highway. I spend an hour or two a week, sometimes much more than that, walking a remote section of the acequia, checking out the dam, trying to figure out what the beavers are up to next, seeing if the lowermost parciantes are getting enough water. I know our side of the little valley and all the people who live there so well I sometimes wish I could forget about it all. Sometimes it seems like a curse, a burden, this great stone that weighs down my life—but most of the time I know better, that this place is me, it is my life, it is what will make meaning out of my short existence, and whenever I go somewhere else it is almost all I can think of and talk about and is the only place I can dream of returning to.

And not just that. It's the hills and mountains all around, and even though I don't know them well, and the streams and rivers, I know that they give something to many others like what they give to me—and the almost unbearable light that seems at times as if the whole universe is attempting to illuminate this corner of the world, a light that makes parts of even Los Alamos and Española seem stunning beyond bearing. In such light, under such skies, how can you not plant a garden, plant trees and flowers, plant whole fields? How can you not know that this place is something extraordinary, in the way it strikes through the eye season after season, and makes nearly everywhere else seem tame and subdued or overcrowded and polluted or dark and damp. . . .

■

Suddenly everyone goes Ooh-ah. Course Two has arrived.

Even I have to admit that this is spectacular. It's a bowl of soup. But what a bowl of soup. Imagine this: a shallow white bowl with the left hand filled with bright green soup and the right hand filled with bright red soup, perfect half-moons each, and a lightning-like squiggle of white cream dashing back and forth across the even straight line that divides so perfectly the two hemispheres. The menu reads:

PALAMINO SOUP with GOAT CHEESE CREMA
Two-Color soup of
Roasted New Mexico Green Chile
and Sweet Red Bell Peppers
COYOTE CAFÉ

We all wonder aloud how they managed to pour the two soups into the bowl so as to come out evenly together in a straight line down the middle. Kingsley: "There's a room somewhere filled with messy failures." We all laugh. We dip in. The green side is hot but you can run back to the red to cool down. Delicious, yes, and what fun to scramble up something beautiful, just like little kids, and then get to eat it too.

Some weeks later at the Farmers' Market I run into Mark Miller, impresario of the Coyote Café, and ask him how they get the line straight. "Easy," he says, "just pour the two soups in slowly at the same time."

Back at the farm Rose Mary and daughter Kate and Kiva would be breaking for lunch, wearily bumping around the kitchen, throwing a hastily put together meal on the round oak table stained bright red. They'll be staring into the long afternoon of bunching the statice flowers picked in the morning. The free lunch invitation said only one person per farm but I notice a few ignored the rule, as I should have. Rose Mary would have enjoyed this.

"Adjudication," I announce, trying to pick up where we left off, "is where everything finally comes to a boil."

"Now explain that to me," Jerilou demands.

But where to begin? Where to end. Adjudication. Adjudication of water rights, which apparently never ends.

"Adjudication is the real threat to the north," I plunge in, "because it ends up separating land and water and turns water into something that can be bought and sold separate from the land—and thus shipped out of the north."

"Wait a minute," Kingsley stops me. "How does this start?"

"It's a legal process the object of which is to establish clear title to water rights, usually triggered by the state's involvement in some Federal or interstate water project. It takes the form of a lawsuit. The plaintiff is the State Engineer Office which is charged with managing water in New Mexico. What happens when a stream system is adjudicated is that each water user—and we're talking about surface water rights of streams and rivers not underground aquifers—is served with an offer of judgment by the court. This offer of judgment is in terms of acre feet per year, the right to use so many acre feet of water per year. The State Engineer makes you an offer on the basis of your past water use and other factors, in terms of so many acre feet per year. You can accept the offer or you can go to court and contest it and say, for example, no, I have the right to twice that many acre feet per year."

"Well, fine," says Kingsley. "What's the matter with that?"

"All kinds of things. Just to start with, look at the unit of measure, the acre foot. It's not a unit of measure we experience, there's no acre foot of water back at the Bureau of Standards in Washington that we can go look at. Nonetheless it shares a characteristic of other units of measure established and enforced by government regulation, that of absoluteness. An acre foot is water sufficient to cover about 43,500 square feet in water one foot deep.

"This may seem an obscure quibble. What I want to emphasize is not the acre foot's peculiarity as a unit of measure so much as its absoluteness. The weather, however, is not absolute. It changes. Some years are wet, some are dry. And the global climate is changing faster than ever before in recorded time. An absolute measure of water pinned to an increasingly fluctuating source of water, the weather, would seem to court becoming irrelevant in very short order.

"By contrast acequias apportion water to their members on the basis of a variable share. If there's lots of water in the river, then your share is large. If the river's dry, your share is unfortunately worthless as long as the condition lasts. And acequias along a section of a river or stream will usually have long-standing traditional agreements on how to divide the water up during dry years. Which leads to the second major problem with adjudication."

"Which is?" Jerilou asks, looking up from her bowl, which she is scraping clean.

"One of the things the adjudication process does is to assign what are called priority dates to each ditch. In large part priority dates are based on historical documentation. The ditch which has the oldest piece of paper gets all the water in a dry year, doesn't have to share with anyone else. The priority date system wipes out longstanding oral traditions that in some cases have dealt with water shortages over hundreds of years. It creates a winner-take-all situation. Essentially when the adjudication process is completed—when in fact it can ever be completed at all, which is another problem—what you have done is to replace a largely oral tradition, in which a variable supply of water is negotiated among all parties, with its exact opposite, which is a rigid system based on an absolute unit of measure and in which the notions of negotiation and sharing have been completely removed. In some sense this is supposed to be 'progress.'"

A pause during which I catch up with my soup. Finally Jerilou asks. "But if it's not progress, then why go through with it all?"

"Part of it is about regional water management and distribution among Colorado, New Mexico, and Texas. The acre foot as a unit of measure is convenient in administrative terms for managing large quantities of water, when they can be managed. The federal government is the ultimate force driving adjudication, because it wants interstate claims to be resolved, for the sake of its large water projects. Interstate agreements, such as the San Juan Diversion Project, which piped water under the mountains of Colorado into the reservoirs of northern New Mexico, kicked off the notorious Aamodt water adjudication suit which has gone on for twenty years at a cost of millions, and with divisive consequences for the Indian Pueblos and the neighboring Hispanic and Anglo communities of Nambé, Pojoaque, Tesuque, and San Ildefonso.

"Yet there's a fallacy in all of this having to do with projections about the weather, as I said. The big suit that the State of New Mexico recently agreed to settle with Texas over the Pecos River had to do with the fact that the Pecos River refused to run as predicted. Long-range predictions of any kind, everybody is beginning to understand, are very tricky. Administrators want things to be tied down and fixed for all time. But water isn't like that."

The green side of the soup is even hotter than I thought. I have to pause for oral ventilation. Unfortunately I have eaten up all of the red side of the soup. And leaving one's plate not licked clean will definitely be noticed. They're all here, happily prowling around: Pranzo's Rick Post, Coyote Café's Mark Miller, and a couple of others I haven't met. I will proceed by quarter spoonfuls and copious drinks of water.

"But the worst effect of adjudication is the one I mentioned before, that it allows water to be separated from the land. Under Spanish water law, you couldn't do that. You could lose your water rights by failing to use them but you couldn't sell them off separately. Today, now, in New Mexico, once your water rights have been adjudicated, you end up with a title, as it were, which you can sell to, say, a developer down here in Santa Fe or Albuquerque. The river and the ditch stay where they are up in the foothills or the mountains, in your back yard or front yard or wherever. What happens is that by selling you lose the right to take water from either."

A rise in the level of hubbub in the restaurant causes us all to look around. Blood-sugar level is up, people are reviving, laughter is passing from table to table. I raise my voice. "Which leads to another problem.

Ditches don't own water rights, they contol only the distribution of the water that passes down their channels. But if you're on an acequia and you sell your water rights, then the ditch loses a member, loses a share, loses the right to distribute that share of water, loses your contribution in labor and money toward the operation of the ditch, and thus becomes weaker in proportion. In effect when you sell your water rights you are also selling something that doesn't belong to you, you are selling a portion of your community's commons. An equivalent situation would be that of a taxpayer who holds, in some manner of speaking, shares in the community school system or the highways or the gas and power and phone lines—systems we all pay for and use and benefit from without actually owning—but who is allowed to sell his 'share' of these things for his private profit."

I'm down to the last spoonfuls of the green chile soup, tongue deadened but apparently still functional. "The adjudication process does not take into account the community value of a water right, the commons portion of it. This has to do with how the State Engineer and the courts regard water—as dictated by legislative statute. They regard water as property, as a commodity that enables material production and consumption. I am not denying those values. I am saying that the community value, the commons value of water, is what is being ignored in the adjudication process. This is why adjudication is such a threat to the traditional landscape of northern New Mexico. It is the first step in their eventual destruction."

The next course is here, apparently a salad cut out of very fine green lace arranged in a roseate pattern on a small plate. The menu reads:

FRESH GARDEN SALAD
Sun-dried Tomato and Piñon Vinaigrette
LA CASA SENA

The greenery at first puzzles me. Then I decide it's probably endive. I wish they had provided a list of who supplied the produce. This looks like something out of old Truman Brigham's garden up in Española, the endive at least. He's been farming up there since the 1930s when the Denver, Rio Grande and Western narrow gauge trains of what was nicknamed the Chile Line were still running through the valley twice a day to and from their southern terminus a block away from here, the old brick station now housing Tomasita's Restaurant. Truman went into farming full time when he retired as a Highway Department gardener twenty years ago. When I'm his age I hope I'm still going as strong as he is.[7]

"Destructive?" Jerilou wants to know. "I can see that, yeah, you take away the water and people's fields dry up, but not everybody's, right?"

"But look at the process by which that happens. Adjudication suits are carried out by stream and therefore by community. Imagine what happens when suddenly everyone in a village receives an offer of judgment. The legal process is inherently adversarial to begin with. The legal system is a place we usually go to when all else fails, when dialogue and mediation break down. Putting into motion legal machinery almost automatically excludes those theoretically prior possibilities of discussion and mediation or other forms of truth-seeking. The State Engineer has at his disposal hydrologists, aerial surveys, historians, and other expert witnesses, plus lots of lawyers, plus a healthy budget appropriated year after year by the State Legislature. What do you have in the village targeted for adjudication? A lot of scared and suspicious neighbors who probably don't fully understand what is happening to them in all its complexity and what is about to be done to their community, people easily intimidated by the power of any governmental agency. And things become horribly complicated if one of the co-defendants is one of the several arms of the federal government itself with its own claims on water rights, such as the Forest Service, the Bureau of Land Management, or the Bureau of Indian Affairs which is administrative warden of every tribal nation in the country. This will bring in the resources of the Department of the Interior, the Department of Agriculture, the Department of Justice, one and all. Your village dweller's co-defendant, the Federal Government of the United States of America, has of course lots of money and lots of lawyers. Things get really interesting in what is called the *inter se* stage of an adjudication suit, which is when each and every defendant can contest the claims of each and every other defendant. Which means that your low-income landowner, who may already have battles going with the welfare office or the food stamp office or Medicare or Social Security or all four, now has to take on not only the State Engineer Office, who is suing him, but also potentially each and every one of his fellow defendants, which include a lot of relatives and all his neighbors and the Forest Service, BLM and BIA, and do so with money scraped out of his own pocket.[8] There is obviously something very wrong here. In social terms this could be described as a state of chaos."

I caution myself in my over-excitement to chew my endive very carefully in order to avoid a repetition of an embarrassing choking incident that took place in a student restaurant in the basement of the Faculté de Médecine on the rue de Saints-Pères in Paris thirty years ago, which I vividly recall in a blushing flash.

"The point is that adjudication sooner or later turns into a legal free-for-all pitting neighbor against neighbor, poor against rich, citizen against his own government, and goes on for years, costing a fortune in legal fees, all to clear the way for the liquidation of a community asset in order to 'rationalize' water distribution. I doubt you could conceive of a more disastrous social policy for rural northern New Mexico even if you deliberately set out to do so. And yet, for all this, as a last argument, adjudication doesn't really seem to work."

A sudden thrusting of plates in front of us announces the arrival of the main course. Imagine a bi-colored dumpling in the shape of a triangularly folded napkin, about two-thirds of the seamless form a baked dough color and the other third dark blue-black. How on earth did they do that? A friend later tells me that she heard they dipped the dumpling in culinary grade squid ink. We all read:

BLACK & WHITE PASTA TRIANGLES
Filling of Red and Green Chili,
Seared New Potatoes
and Mozzarella, topped with smokey Chipotle and Arugula
SANTACAFE

"What's Chipotle?"
"I don't know."

"Seared potatoes?" I wonder out loud. I notice that the writer of this menu item used the Texas and outside-world spelling, *chili*, not the New Mexican spelling, *chile*. Maybe that battle has been lost in Santa Fe. My impression is that Taos is still putting up fierce resistance.

We launch in with knife and fork. Tasty, interesting, on first bite, but the sort of dish you need to suspend judgment on until the last bite. Nobody is raving, calling out Delicious, Scrumptious, I'm Going to Have Seconds.

"Your last argument," Kingsley reminds me, hopefully. Did I hear emphasis on *last*?

"We won't hold you to that," says Jerilou with a forgiving smile.

"All I wanted to say was that up in Taos and the Red River there are areas that are being re-adjudicated because the first time around the State Engineer Office missed about fifteen hundred acres and some three hundred and fifty landowners. Adjudication suits going on now in Taos involve some five thousand landowners, plus not a few who will try to ignore the whole business in the hope that it will simply go away or because they're deservedly suspicious of the whole thing.

"Now it's true that there have been special one-time appropriations for non-subsidized defendants in the Aamodt case. Congress voted a couple of million to give them a hand. Northern New Mexico Legal Services, whose board I'm on, helps out. But our whole annual budget for all types of low-income civil administrative and legal problems is less than a million for all of northern New Mexico, from Gallup to Las Vegas and north, and we have a policy about not getting into the middle of fights between two groups of low-income people, such as the Pueblo tribes and Hispanic landowners, so there's a limit to what we can do."

At this point Harvey Frauenglass gets up, explaining he has to be in Albuquerque by 2:30. "I'm going to have to miss dessert," he protests.

"Can we save your portion?" I suggest. "I'll leave it under a napkin next door to your parking space at the Farmers' Market."

Harvey guffaws and waves goodbye. Yesterday the market vice-president, Arnold Souder, a retired mining engineer, went out to Harvey's place in Embudo with another board member, Pamela Roy, and filled the back of his station wagon with fourteen bushel boxes of ground-fall apples to take back to one of the soup kitchens for the homeless in Santa Fe. By the end of the year Arnold estimates that this particular soup kitchen will serve 70,000 meals. By the end of the year he will have personally delivered about 10,000 pounds of produce either donated by farmers at the Farmers' Market or which he has driven out to farms to collect. The soup kitchen he delivers stuff to, the one run by St. John the Baptist Catholic Church, is one of four or five such places in Santa Fe. Santa Fe's a hard place to be poor. Rents are high because of the pressures of development and gentrification. This translates into a certain number of low income people being squeezed out into the condition of homelessness. The local branch of the welfare office has a reputation for being notoriously inept. Some weeks ago a Legal Services attorney, Patricia Glaszek, spoke at length to the board about a class action suit against the welfare department on behalf of clients who had been denied benefits for trivial infractions of capricious rules. A few of us asked her about how the welfare department was run. "Is it ineptitude or evil?" I asked. She said it was hard to know, that the office has a staff turnover rate of 25% a year, that it takes three months to train new staff, and that the starting salary is $7500 a year, which qualifies some new welfare department employees for food stamps themselves. At the end of her talk she asked whether we had any more questions. I remarked that I was afraid to ask.

All this was swirling around my mind in the eddies of Harvey's departure, amid the clink of silverware and the gabble of dozens of conversations, in this warm moment of safe enclosure, in the sort of restaurant that makes being well-heeled in Santa Fe so pleasant and easy.

Jerilou brings me back to the moment. "But who's paying? Who's paying for this adjudication business?"

"You. Me. The Taxpayer. Which includes the very people who will suffer from its effects. And we are, remember, a regressive tax state in which the poor pay a disproportionate share of taxes."

"Sure," she says. "But what can you do about it? Where do you start?"

That's the hard one. It always is. "I don't know. You have to educate people, first of all, as always. Most people probably think that the adjudication of water rights, whatever that is, is just fine. It's a kind of legal housekeeping, something to do with making sure boundaries and fence-lines are where they're supposed to be, something like that. But what we're really dealing with is social policy—consciously planned or not—disguised as something else. It's fair to say that nobody at any level has been given the choice to vote for or against the radical changes that the adjudication process will ultimately bring down on the rural landscape of northern New Mexico. Santa Fe and Taos live increasingly off tourist revenues, yet one of the tourists assets that will be consumed is that very landscape, in the form of traditional villages and agricultural valleys of the north. To proceed with adjudication in the present manner will move both water and people to the cities, to Taos, to Santa Fe, Albuquerque, and Las Cruces. Does anybody besides urban developers really want this?

"Legislative action would force the matter to public attention. You could, for example, propose to cut the funding of that portion of the State Engineer Office that is devoted to adjudication suits, pending an independent and objective study of the whole question. Federal pressure to continue the adjudication process can be resisted if, at the state level, someone, or enough of us, stand up and say that it's not working, it's destroying something of value, it's absurdly expensive, and doesn't work anyway."

The eating remains serious while we try to figure out the contents of the dumpling and pick out which is the chipotle—or is that the sauce?—and which the arugula. My mind slips forward to the tasks that lie in wait for me, to the drive home, to wondering whether I'll need to eat dinner after this meal, perhaps only something quick and light around 5:30. Then our daughter Kate and Kiva and I will carry some empty boxes out to the basil patch in front of the sheds and snip off four or five boxes full of shoots, sending up a cloud of fragrance in the warm, still air, and then carry the basil back to the work table to bunch and wash, packing the wet bunches back into the forty-year-old wooden apple boxes and sliding them into the back of the pickup. Then I'll walk down to the orchard where this morning's picking of Walla Walla sweet onions lie like bulbous fishes in their boxes in the loader of the bright orange tractor, in the shade of an apple tree, at the edge of the lawn. I'll drive them up and transfer them into the camper and then cover the lower layer of boxes with a half dozen planks painted sky blue which will become the countertop of my market stand the next morning, in a pine grove a stone's throw from what was the site of the very first lab buildings at Los Alamos. Then on top of the planks in the camper will go a dozen bushel baskets of statice flowers in bunches, seven to a basket, each bunch dressed up in a filmy wrapping of spun polyester. Then, as the sun slips below the bluff to the west and the sky begins to darken, I'll check that the scales and cash box and sacks are still in the truck and put in a lug box of garlic, a half-dozen of Rose Mary's garlic arrangements, display flats, a water jug, two tool boxes, and then I'll turn the truck around so as to be facing out for the early morning departure, roll up the windows, set the heater to high and clean the windshield.

"There is some hope in all this," I finally suggest. "People are more aware now than they used to be, more willing to organize and fight. The people of Taos stopped the Indian Camp Dam, which is what John Nichols's *Milagro Beanfield War* was about, a project that would have speeded up the whole process that adjudication unleashes, that of transferring land and water rights from small subsistence farmers, largely Hispanic, to bigger operations and developers, largely Anglo. Ten years ago the Bureau of Reclamation cooked up a plan to put a dam across the Rio Grande in Velarde and run a canal right through the village and up on to the flats toward Alcalde, to carry water to arid land owned by an Española developer. The San Juan Pueblo was used as a front for all this, I believe. Nobody knew about it until the survey crews arrived one day and started driving stakes in people's yards. The public outcry was enough to kill the project, which would have had serious effects on the water table of the whole Velarde basin.

"And then there was the notorious Phreatophyte Eradication Program which proposed to cut down all the cottonwoods and tamarisks[9] and willows along the Rio Grande for two hundred plus miles between Elephant Butte Dam and Velarde."

"You're kidding," Kingsley insists.

"What was the point of that?" Jerilou wants to know.

"Phreatophytes are trees that pump moisture into the air. On a hot dry day you can stand underneath a cottonwood and feel an exceedingly fine spray of water. The idea was that by cutting down all the vegetation from Velarde to Truth or Consequences there would be more water in the river for big irrigation projects of the Mesilla Valley, in the Las Cruces area. Hence the Phreatophyte Eradication Program. Fortunately they never went through with it."[10]

"I can't believe this."

"But anyway, because people are more alert to this kind of nonsense than they used to be they've got organized and stayed organized over the years, particularly up in Taos where some of the hotter adjudication issues are being worked over. And fortunately we've got a Legal Services attorney up there, Fred Waltz, who's been working with people up there for years and who's come up with some innovative strategies. Lately he's managed to get some of the traditional oral water sharing agreements among acequias written into the final decrees, which is a move in the right direction to undermine the insidious priority date system. It isn't much, but it's a glimmer."[11]

Waitresses are skimming empty dinner plates from tables and replacing them with smaller dessert plates. A sudden wave of bustling activity in the place indicates what my watch tells me, that we are running somewhat behind schedule. Dessert is usually self-evident, as this one, or these ones, prove to be, two thin slices of pie. We study our menus for the taxonomical details.

FRESH LEMON TART WITH PECAN CRUST
CHOCOLATE GANACHE TART with PECAN CRUST
Award Winner—"Taste of Santa Fe"
NECTARINE

The lemon tart, which I launch into first, a kind of meringue, tastes a little eggy to me but is made up for by the sensational chocolate slice, distinctly prize-winning, yes. We are all absorbed. One does not talk through dessert. There is not much of it. It could be gobbled down thoughtlessly, without truly experiencing it, with the mind on other things. We were all too full to claim absent Harvey's dessert during that moment the waitress hesitated before not putting it down at his abandoned place-setting but soon regret it.

Coffee is being poured. People are standing up, stretching, moving about, running over to the tables they wish they had sat at, hailing old friends. The Hammetts are both fidgety and glassy-eyed. I have that thirsty, half-gasping sensation in the throat that tells me I have talked too much. There is nothing more to say. A faint sadness overcomes me, the sense that the wave of words has risen higher and higher to a crest, only to crash down into a silence of doubts that all is finally nothing more than talk. Can talk finally ever do any good at all?

Well, anyway, it was a nice lunch. And free, too.

Gerald Chacón, Santa Fe County Agricultural Extension Agent, who will introduce the after-lunch speakers, including myself, is positioning himself near a far wall, perhaps to figure out how we are to address a room divided in half by a peekaboo wall. He is a short roly-poly man with bright dark eyes and a ready smile, dressed in the regulation agricultural bureaucrat's khakis, cowboy boots, and ten-gallon hat. I pat my shirt pocket. The page of typed remarks is still there. A feeble shot of adrenaline struggles vainly against the swamping inertia of digestion.

A quick dash to the john is called for. I excuse myself. It too is all angles, but with mirrors. At first I wonder whether I have stepped into the right room. Some elegant porcelain umbrella-stand things occupy two corners. I am about to ask another patron, "Is this the men's room?" when I realized the umbrella stands are urinals. Wonders never cease. I eye them as markers or monuments denoting the great distances I have come today from my habitual Wednesday afternoon life, the far point, the ultimate limit, the goal posts of the final turn, after which I will be sent swinging back, faster and faster, to where I have come from and where I know I belong. I conclude and flush.

Back at the table three conversations are going on at once while across the room Gerald Chacón is waving his arms. I sit down. Jerilou picks up the tape recorder and hands it to Kingsley, deep in conversation with someone at the next table, and looks up at me and says:

"This was great. But you know what?" She flashes me her dimply, toothsome smile. Her launching-the-ships smile. I suppose I could have guessed what was coming. "You know, Kingsley and I think you really ought to write the article yourself. You're the one to do it."[12]

Over the din of seventy people laughing and shouting, Gerald Chacón calls out, "Can I have your attention please?"

|1994| *Author's Note:* Other than grammatical errors, the following letter remains as sent in 1994, rhetorical excesses and all. The letter was widely discussed within the State Engineer Office and at a water conference and was reprinted in two environmental newsletters. However, no official answer was ever forthcoming. Many of the issues it raises have been rendered even more urgent by the passage of time.

AN OPEN LETTER TO THE STATE ENGINEER
El Bosque Garlic Farm
PO Box 56
Dixon, NM 87527
Ph: 579 4288
April 20, 1994
Mr. Eluid L. Martinez
State Engineer
State Engineer Office
State of New Mexico
Bataan Memorial Building, Room 101
Post Office Box 25102
Santa Fe, NM 87505–5102

Dear Mr. Martinez:

I am writing to ask you to consider a question, or a series of questions, which have been building up in urgency in my mind. I have reason to believe that I am not alone in my concern.

The questions have to do with water—which is to say

with its numberless companions of culture, community, tradition, history, and fauna and flora.

I am writing to you because you are, as State Engineer, the water master for us all, the keeper of the keys and seals, and the one we look to as the knower of all secrets of this most mysterious substance. You may argue that I attribute far too much power to your office— but I do so in order to suggest how powerless those of us who live in small rural communities now feel regarding most questions of water.

For my part I am writing as a farmer, as a mayordomo of one acequia, as a commissioner or another, and as a writer. The question that comes back to worry me every year at this time when we begin digging out the acequias of the Embudo Valley is a simple one: how do we save them? I don't mean in the small, specific sense. I know the answer to that. The answer is always to get out and do the work, help it get done, dig out the acequia, and bring the water down. I have done that in one form or another for the past twenty-two years.

But in the larger sense of the acequias as a system, as a feature of the cultural landscape, how do we save them from being engulfed by the rising tidal wave of social change?

I think in particular of the many small traditional acequias which serve to knit together the countless river valley communities of northern New Mexico. I don't know the exact number, but I have heard the figures 800 to 1200 spoken of, and I assume the majority of these are to be found in the northern half of the state.

I take for granted the reasons why they should be saved, and I hope you share in these. I believe they should be saved because they are repositories of a unique tradition of rural self-governance with few parallels elsewhere in rural America. As gravity-fed irrigation systems they are simple, energy efficient, and ecologically sound, and their hand-dug watercourses serve to expand the riparian habitats from which they flow. As systems serving small parcels of arable land, they have proven historically sustainable over centuries in a way that grander irrigation works never have and perhaps never will, anywhere in the world. And because they make few claims on the public works budgets compared to other features of the rural infrastructure, employing local, indeed, neighborhood labor almost exclusively, they may eventually prove to be valuable models for future small scale, self-governing institutions in rural areas. Finally I take for granted, as I trust you do, that the acequias are one of the central institutions of Hispanic culture in northern New Mexico, and that their extinction would be an irrecoverable cultural loss.

I also believe that with modest encouragement acequias can overcome the latest challenges of social change. Their traditions have proven adaptable to an extraordinary degree over the course of their history, enabling them to jump both the Mediterranean and the Atlantic, and pass through two and three major language changes, to root in New Mexico, with the help of Native American ways, quite as if they were invented here.

But if they are to survive what is becoming the greatest challenge ever to their existence, I believe they will need help—and fast—in the following ways:

1. THE TRUE PUBLIC AND PRIVATE COSTS, IN FINANCIAL AND SOCIAL TERMS, OF WATER RIGHTS ADJUDICATION CASES, MUST BECOME A MATTER OF PUBLIC DEBATE.

Acequias are under siege everywhere. The story varies from village to village, valley to valley, but in essence it is very much the same—the well-financed forces of real estate development in all its forms, regulated and unregulated, are moving too fast for the good of most communities that are being subjected to their ways.

It can be argued that the adjudication of water rights, when carried out in the present climate of over-heated real estate development and speculation, will only aggravate the problem by placing an unreasonable burden of expense on private landowners and public agencies—and in ways that ultimately exclude more creative, less confrontational solutions.

The Aamodt suit is the classic case. Estimates of public and private costs over the past 27 years of the still unresolved suit, which holds the dubious distinction of being the oldest on the Federal docket, run at $40 million, which averages out to $40,000 per parcel of land of the 1000 parcels in the suit—or over $13,000 per irrigated acre.[13]

At a recent meeting I was told by a member of your staff that $20 million was to be budgeted for the adjudication of the waters of the Rio Grande from San Juan to Pilar, and the Rio Embudo up to Santa Barbara, some 40 miles of watercourse. This presumably was the state portion of the cost and did not include the budgets of those Federal agencies involved, nor what private landowners would spend in legal costs defending their water right claims. I think it is safe to say that we are looking at another $40 million water rights suit to be carried out over a generation or more.

If no changes are made in the process of establishing water rights claims through the courts, and considering the costs of all past and future adjudication suits, I would estimate that well over $100 million will be spent in public and private money in northern New Mexico by the time any of these suits are settled, if any of them ever are

2. AT THE VERY LEAST A COST-BENEFIT ANALYSIS SHOULD BE PERFORMED ON PUBLIC EXPENDITURES OF THIS MAGNITUDE.

Most of the money spent on the adjudication process goes not to the rural communities themselves but into the hands of state, federal, and private attorneys, hydrologists, surveyors, historians, and a supporting army of urban bureaucrats, while the unfortunate rural landowners who have claims to water rights are submitted to a protracted, divisive, and expensive legal process which ends, in theory, in their possessing a marketable water right which can be sold independent of their land. The ultimate effect of the adjudication process is to allow land to be separated from water, with complex consequences at the local level, the most tragic of which will be the liquidation of the acequia system itself.

I have long argued that the fatal flaw of the adjudication process is that it allows the "commons value" of a water right to be privatized away and dissipated. Much of the commons value of water resides in the acequia system, which conveys the water from the river to the individual landowner. When that landowner is allowed to sell off his water right, he is also selling something which does not properly belong to him as an individual property owner, in the form of that portion of a commons which until then has underpinned and sustained the equity of his property as land and water. When an acequia loses a water right, it also loses a member, a ratepayer, a laborer. It is as if, as a property owner and taxpayer, I am given the right to sell my "share" of the local commons in the form of the railing of the highway bridge or a shelf of books in the library of the public school. In most spheres of public life we spend much effort separating the private from what we hold publicly in common as citizens, but here the adjudication process fails to acknowledge the existence of an important commons—which should never be subject to the market forces that adjudication ultimately releases. An acequia is the collective creation of generation after generation of parciantes, and it belongs not to any one parciante, but to all future generations. If anything, the state should be a vigorous defendant of this commons, not the destroyer of it.

For many people it is becoming a scandal that the state has committed so much in the way of resources to what, in the end, will be seen to have been an expensive, socially disruptive, and culturally destructive process—startlingly parallel to what took place during the reign of the infamous Santa Fe Ring a hundred years ago, when many Hispanic communities were stripped of their land grants by scheming Anglo lawyers in the Court of Private Land Claims. Whether the intention was originally there or not, the State Engineer Office seems deeply engaged in an experiment in massive social engineering.

3. ACEQUIAS MUST PARTICIPATE IN DECISIONS AFFECTING WATER USE AT ALL LEVELS OF GOVERNMENT—MUNICIPAL, COUNTY, STATE, AND FEDERAL.

The network of acequias which cover much of Northern New Mexico is difficult to define as a coherent system because of the idiosyncratic independence of the almost microscopic governmental bodies that make up the whole. In their fragmentation lie both their

strength and weakness. Many people have advocated that the acequias organize themselves in order to obtain what they need for their
survival. But the problem is a little like "organizing" the poor—
whose condition is primarily characterized by lack of organization.
The fragmentation of the acequias and the urgency of mustering
local participation leaves little time and energy for acequia officials
to contemplate the larger view—and as every volunteer knows, time
on the road, meals in town, and phone calls never get reimbursed.

A central problem here is that though acequias are defined as
governmental bodies they lack—because of their smallness—
the institutional tools and bridges that might enable them to inter-
act more fruitfully with other governmental entities. The top-down
urban bias of agencies mandated to assist acequias, notably your
office, the Interstate Stream Commission, and the Corps of Engineers, perpetuates a chasm blocking the free flow of ideas and infor-
mation. By now, at this late date, I would expect these agencies (plus
municipalities and counties) to be working with active advisory
committees of acequia representatives from all over the state. As far
as I know, none do.

The recent formation of the State Acequia Commission may
eventually prove to be a step in the right direction—largely depending, in my view, on whether or not it can acquire a genuine rural
constituency, and whether it can create solutions derived from that
constituency rather than from the needs of the urban bureaucratic
establishment of Santa Fe.[14]

4. ACEQUIAS MUST BE INVESTED IN AT THE LOCAL LEVEL.

The State Acequia Commission, or your office, cannot save the
acequias, or even local communities, unless we are collectively prepared to invest in them. Investing in them means integrating them
into the networks of public taxation and finance and technical assistance at the local and state level, so that acequias can avail themselves of the public power to which they are entitled—without
sacrificing their local character and independence.

At present there are several programs through state and federal agencies to assist acequias in capital projects—rebuilding diversion dams, headgates, and other structures. Lacking, however, are programs of technical assistance for acequia management, particularly in the areas of clerical assistance, accounting procedures and in the maintaining of records and archives—an area where acequias are particularly vulnerable.

The acequias are sufficiently central to most rural communities that they would be well served by the establishment of part-time local or on-site watershed offices, whose staff could assist in record-keeping problems, record security, and even perform banking or credit union services. I do not believe such offices should be under the control of the State Engineer Office, but such offices could also assist in the gathering and filing of various declarations and forms concerning water rights and acequia management. Such offices would also serve to decentralize overhead budgets now concentrated in cities.

5. ACEQUIA WORKERS AND PAID OFFICIALS MUST BE MORE FULLY COMPENSATED FOR THEIR LABORS.

In the case of paid mayordomos and other paid acequia workers, it should be acknowledged that their work is indeed labor and therefore qualifying for those protections and benefits presumably afforded by law to all workers, such as Workman's Compensation, Unemployment Insurance, Social Security, and (as public employees, employed by a subdivision of the State of New Mexico) state retirement benefits.

The hitch here is of course the burden of paperwork that would swamp any volunteer commission I know of, but this is precisely what the local field offices above would help deal with. The alternative, which is unfortunately the preferred model of the day, is to further marginalize paid mayordomos and workers by declaring them contract workers—or not workers at all—or simply by legally excluding them from most such programs, as in the case of agricultural workers.

There is a more positive model in the way the State Fire Marshall's Office can award modest pensions to volunteer firemen after twenty years of service. The point may be not a question of the amount of money so much as the acknowledgment of public service—which incidentally, in the case of volunteer fire departments, serves to maintain property values and hold down the cost of fire insurance. Acequia officials and active parciantes, it needs to be said, also do much to maintain the value of rural real estate.

At present we relegate acequias to the underground economy of flea markets and garage sales. Through neglect acequias have undergone a process of de facto privatization in some respects. You might say we are getting exactly what we are paying for. Or, more exactly, the true costs of running acequias are being carried on the backs of those rural people either so committed or so foolish or desperate enough to assume such burdens. By bringing hidden or subsidized costs to the surface in the form of fair wages and appropriate social benefits, at least to a partial degree, I believe we could increase local participation by adding positive incentives, thereby raising the morale of those who perform the actual managerial and physical labor. I can think of no better way to bring acequias back into a position of being respected institutions at the center of rural life.

The crisis of the acequia is one of participation at all levels. I argue that if acequias are invited not into the courtroom later but to the conference table and meeting room first, to help craft strategies and decisions early on that will shape their existence and the existence of their many small communities, then at all levels, from the neighborhood up, they will recover the fullness of their potential as exemplary institutions of local self-governance.

I hope you will consider this letter as a call to your office to begin redirecting its resources from the current task of dividing and destroying to the more creative work of rebuilding and healing.

Sincerely yours,
[signed]
Stanley Crawford
Mayordomo, Acequia del Bosque, Dixon;
President, Commission of the Acequia del Llano, Dixon;
President, Board of Directors,
Santa Fe Area Farmers' Market, Santa Fe

|2000| Halfway into John Ford's classic 1940s film, *The Grapes of Wrath*, the camera pans across some adobe houses and a church, behind which rises a wooded arroyo. What you don't see in the film is how the arroyo rises and opens out into a wooded basin of some eighty acres, source of two thin flows of water that stream down behind the church.

The village in the film was San Antonio de Padua, seven miles east and 1500 feet above Albuquerque, tucked back into a saddle of land, at the bottom of a rumpled mantle of juniper-piñon woodland that rises gently to the west. Four miles above the village the slope crests at the 10,000-foot South Sandia Peak, one of the promontories of the Sandia Range that overlooks Albuquerque below.

Once a fleeting backdrop to a film about dispossessed sharecroppers, San Antonio became the center of its own drama of dispossession fifty years later when a real estate development above the old village threatened the source of its water and the traditions that have governed its use for the past 150 years. Established by the Spanish in 1819, the village is one of a string of settlements on the Turquoise Trail, now NM Highway 14 and commonly known as the "back way" between Santa Fe and Albuquerque. In earlier times the stream through San Antonio served local Pueblo Indians, Apache bands, gringo traders, and Union soldiers regrouping after the 1862 Battle of Glorieta Pass. Eventually the trail became a road. In the 1970s it was widened into a four lane highway to serve the needs of the commuters who were fast populating the bedroom suburbs of Cedar Crest, Sandia Park, and Sandia Knolls, whose higher altitude and airy scrub forests were luring them up out of the heat of Albuquerque.

The new highway cruelly bisected the old village, which is no longer recognizable as such. What is left is a scattering of adobe houses and mobile homes. San Antonio's three plazas are now memories, most of its buildings have crumbled back to earth, intermingling with the shards of the earlier pueblo occupants.

Yet something of the spirit of the old village has survived in its colonial water use traditions. Above, in the wooded basin now known as Los Manzanares, two small springs feed the twin silvery ribbons of a tiny irrigation ditch system operated under traditional Spanish water law. It serves some sixty San Antonio properties, providing a dozen families with a source of clean drinking water.

The ditch is known as the Acequia Madre de San Antonio de Padua. The term *acequia* is Arabic, dating back to the Moorish occupation of Spain; it can mean either the ditch channel itself or the organizational structure that governs the ditch and distributes its water. An acequia is managed by a ditch boss or mayordomo, a word of clearly Latin origins, and three comisionados or commissioners, all elected by the landowning members of the acequia.

Spurred on by the looming threat of real estate development, a band of San Antonio activists began reviving neglected acequia traditions in 1985. They were also encouraged by a coalition of Albuquerque land use professionals and the Trust for Public Land Southwest Office, who were seeking ways to protect open space in rapidly sprawling Bernalillo County. The end result almost fifteen years later was the preservation of San Antonio's watershed and its acequia from a real estate development that would have disrupted hundreds of years of water use by Hispanic villagers.

As I drive up into a dirt expanse that was once one of San Antonio's plazas, a figure sitting in the shadows of the stuccoed cement-block church stands up and waves. This is Chris Jinzo, a 43-year old who has served as mayordomo of the acequia for the past twelve years. He is a man of medium height wearing a baseball cap, flannel shirt, jeans and black and white running shoes. There is something reserved yet intense about his dark brown eyes.

After I inquire about the origins of his surname, which he can trace back in Spanish land grant documents to 1789, I follow Jinzo on foot up the hill behind the church into the overgrown arroyo, by means of a dirt track. From the depths of the gully there soon comes the sound of rushing water. A few more steps bring us up to a point where the little acequia reveals itself as a small orderly waterfall dropping fifteen feet from a ledge into an old cement-lined basin. The water then exits via a pipe under the dirt track into another cement catchment box, which funnels the water into a long flume to the other side of the arroyo.

There are perhaps a thousand acequias in Northern New Mexico, two of which I know well, and dozens of others which I have some knowledge of, but this is certainly the smallest one I have ever seen. The flow we are looking at, Chris tells us, is about 80 gallons a minute. A wooden sign next to the waterfall warns that "THE COURSE OF DITCHES OR ACEQUIAS ESTABLISHED PRIOR TO JANUARY 20, 1851 SHALL NOT BE DISTURBED." The date refers to one of the first acts of the legislative assembly of the newly created Territory of New Mexico.

It was here on October 6, 1998 that Mayordomo Chris Jinzo and his brother Steve Jinzo, armed with shotguns, faced down developer Mike Knight, who had brought in a front end loader and backhoe to work on the spot where the acequia crosses the steep dirt track up into Los Manzanares. Knight, a ruggedly handsome, motorcycle-riding real estate developer, had purchased the eighty-eight-acre property in 1994. His plans called for the placing of some thirty upscale homesites in the slop-ing basin and on the ridge above it. What he didn't take into account was the determination of a handful of village activists to keep their ancient acequia running clear and free.

■

The confrontation was a scene right out of yet another movie of dispos-session, Robert Redford's *Milagro Beanfield War*, based on the novel by John Nichols. The roots of this particular dispute reach back to the orig-inal Spanish settlement of San Antonio, which was part of the 36,437 hectare Cañon de Carnue Land Grant awarded by the Spanish crown in 1763 but reduced to 2,000 hectares in 1901 by the U. S. Territorial courts. This represented a vast loss of commons land for grazing and wood gathering for the Hispanic residents.

As part of the 1901 settlement, Los Mazanares passed out of the land grant into private hands. Homesteaded in the 1920s, the property was eventually bought by a family by the name of Wright, who built a house and a barn and terraced the sloping basin, and planted trees and row crops. Though old man Wright drove off any villagers from below who tried to enter the property (and who began calling it *La Wrightas*), he respected the village's claim to the spring water and kept the acequia running for the village below. The Wright house burned in the 1970s, leaving a concrete foundation and typical relics of such sites, including the solid remains of a Paramount wood cookstove. From that time on, the villagers reclaimed the property as their de facto commons by gathering apples and pears and other fruit and by keeping the twin channels of the acequia clean.

After the death of Mrs. Wright, the property passed through the hands of two sets of owners, whose plans to develop the property came to nothing. In 1994, Mike Knight, who had built subdivisions all over the East Mountain area, presented his plans for the new development to an unreceptive gathering of villagers in the church parking lot.

We're standing near the concrete foundation of the old Wright house, just above where the dirt track opens out into the miniature valley that was once a thriving farm, now spotted with emerging growths of cottonwood, juniper, piñon, oak and box elder. Jinzo, whose father worked as a caretake for the Wrights, spent his childhood up here. "When you're a kid, you're like Huck Finn. You go do your adventures," he says with a wave toward the enclosing hillsides. The track becomes a path through long yellowing grass toward a clump of old unpruned apple trees, beneath one of which leans a weathered wooden table. Here and there the grass is matted in irregular wide paths, and as we draw close we can see that some of the apple branches have been ripped to the ground. The ample scat under the trees sends a shiver down my spine. Bears. Jinzo tells me that he encountered a 300-pounder around eight o'clock on a summer evening not long ago.

A hundred yards up we come to the second branch of the acequia as it pools around a giant weeping willow whose various trunks occupy an area some twelve feet in diameter. During our return, it becomes clear to me that Jinzo is more than just the mayordomo of the acequia. He knows this little oasis like the back of his hand—and for that matter, probably much of the adjoining Sandia Mountain Wilderness as well. This is where he still conducts his "adventures"—encounters with bears, sightings of hawks and eagles, breaking up dams of sticks and leaves in the diminutive spring-fed channels, repairing spots where bears have knocked down the ditch banks. He is the game warden of the place, the major domo, the head of this particular house of nature, helping keep it clean and quiet and yet functional. He wants to see the orchard restored, he wants to bring school kids up here to show them the acequia, which he calls the "oldest form of government." He wants them to glimpse the deer, elk, bobcats, coyotes, and foxes that move in and out of the property from the adjoining wilderness area that extends all the way up to the crest, he wants them to see their trails and tracks. We have been tramping around this past half hour, I suddenly realize, in his community's outdoor living room.

The first attempts to develop the old Wright property led to the creation of the East Mountain Open Space Commission, founded by Barbara Herrington of nearby Cedar Crest. A constitutionally upbeat and cheerful woman with a degree in planning, Herrington rallied her friends and neighbors to create ". . . a coherent, positive way to fight development, by buying land for preservation. . . ." At the time Bernalillo County had no authority to issue bonds to purchase land, but with the assistance of the Trust for Public Land's Santa Fe office the group organized a successful referendum to amend the state constitution to take care of that barrier in 1996, leading eventually to a bond issue for the purchase of $7 million in open space land.

Although San Antonio de Padua had become something of a Hispanic cultural island in the largely Anglo Cedar Crest area, San Antonio activists were cheered on by the legal and planning support of their neighbors and soon began attending hearings in nearby Tijeras village. They poked into Bernalillo County Courthouse records in Albuquerque and State Engineer Office files in Santa Fe and studied the complex statutes that regulate water use and the governing structures of traditional acequias. They were guided through a number of public hearings by former Albuquerque City Attorney David Campbell. Although water still flowed down the old channels through San Antonio, the organizational structure of the acequia had faded away like the adobe walls of most of the village's buildings. A first step in reviving the acequia as an organization was taken in 1985, when Chris Jinzo became mayordomo, ending a thirty-five-year hiatus.

Descending, we reach the PVC flume on the other side of the gully, where Jinzo explains that some day they will replace it with a more traditional wooden structure. From there on, the northern branch of the acequia, a tiny stream less than a foot wide, travels through the piñon and juniper trees on a shelf dug out of the slope, with a narrow footpath to one side. Perhaps every acequia in Northern New Mexico has charmingly incongruous stretches like this, where the thin flow of water pulls riparian lushness deep into an arid slope of another life zone, in a kind of linear oasis. The grass along the ditch bank has been recently trimmed back. Toward the end of the almost horizontal stretch, which hugs the hillside like a contour line, Jinzo stops us to point out clumps of mint. "Our main drugstore," he observes with a smile. There are three kinds of mint growing along the ditch bank, source of the villagers' *remedios* or traditional potions.

It is late afternoon and almost hot. I pluck a sprig of spearmint and crush the leaves and hold them to my nose. The sharp yet delicate scent revives me. We scramble down a slope and hike back up along the highway back to the church and the car.

Acequia commissioner Gary Hefkin is a warm, enthusiastic fellow in his forties, who commonly leaves one sentence dangling in order to pluck the next thought out of the air. He married into the largely Hispanic community. His wife, Victoria, a handsome, vivacious woman, was born a Gutiérrez and is a land grant heir, as are their two sons, Ian and Joseph. Hefkin can talk about the acequia, "the property," and his adopted community for hours on end with the glee of someone who has found himself in the possession of a historical anomaly that has the power to stop developers in their tracks.

On my first visit to the area with my wife Rose Mary in September, we were regaled with copies of land grant papers and old photographs of the family and the village and glasses of acequia water (as filtered for drinking) in their mobile home on the family property. While Hefkin spun off into the intricacies of recent history, Victoria supplied genealogical details in between minding the boys.

What Hefkin and Jinzo discovered was that acequias were made subdivisions of the state in the 1960s, able to levy taxes and with the powers of eminent domain. Starting in 1993 when the Acequia Madre filed papers with the State Engineer Office, "We went from one declaration of water rights to computers and filing cabinets in five years." By reconstituting the acequia as an organization, it could begin to assert the powers the law had bestowed on it. And given the likelihood that the construction of some twenty-eight 4,000-square-foot houses in and above the little valley of Los Manzanares would have severely degraded the acequia's water quality and exposed its fragile channels to a suddenly dense population of homeowners and their pets, it was clear that the Acequia Madre de San Antonio had grounds to oppose the development of their watershed.

The 1998 standoff between the Jinzo brothers and Knight ended without violence. Both sides had called the county sheriff's office, and by the time the deputies and a county inspector arrived the shotguns were unloaded—if they had ever been loaded in the first place. The county Development Review Department sided with the acequia, pointing out that Knight did not have the appropriate permits to move earth and work on the road. When the confrontation hit the papers, Hefkin told me, offers of assistance poured in from land grant activists all over Northern New Mexico—and even from Old Mexico itself.

Within a generation many of Northern New Mexico's one thousand acequias are likely to find themselves in similar situations. The implications of this victory, achieved by this smallest of acequias, are vast indeed.

■

After the passing of the referendum that allowed the county to buy land, and after the success of the mil levy that provided funding to purchase Los Manzanares, the Trust for Public Land's Project Manager Kelly Huddleston brokered the deal between developer Mike Knight and Bernalillo County. Owing to Knight's determination to subdivide the attractive and potentially profitable property, the negotiations were particularly demanding. But on July 15th, under Huddleston's patient guidance, Knight agreed to a deal and the Trust for Public Land bought the eighty-eight acres of Los Manzanares, immediately conveying the property to the county. Huddleston later reflected that she ". . . was honored to play a role in completing this project, which was so meaningful to the heritage of the people of San Antonio."

Mayordomo Chris Jinzo told me during our walking tour that the community was very pleased by the outcome. Eventually the acequia association hopes to obtain a dedicated easement for its channels.

But now that the property is safely in county hands, it is clearly quite enough for Chris Jinzo and his neighbors to be able to walk up into the hidden valley behind the church, gather a few apples, sit in the grass, dip their hands in the clear water, knowing that this special place once again belongs to all the people of San Antonio de Padua.

|2002| So the wheel turns.

In 1971 when we brought our brush-covered two acres in Dixon, the mayordomo of our acequia was a seventeen-year-old kid more interested in polishing his low-rider than in making the water flow. Thirty years pass. Nearing fifty now, he's back as mayordomo again—but with a much evolved sense of responsibility. And a pickup in place of the low-rider.

I'm entering my fifth or sixth year as being a mere parciante, a landowner member of the acequia, after 25 years of serving as elected commissioner or mayordomo. Which is to say someone who is more interested in when the ditch will be cleaned, when the water will be running again, than in the complicated how. Someone who opens the annual bill with a frown and quick calculations whether it can be paid now or later or even much later.

Yet I can still decode the signs of activity around the acequia this time of year. The pickups parked up at the highway, signaling that a brush-cutting or ditch-cleaning crew is at work somewhere off in the cottonwoods, or is bringing down the water to start the irrigation season. A short convoy of pickups and SUV's down our dirt road means either a special work crew is going to concentrate on one of the perennial trouble spots—or else the commissioners are *andando colectando,* collecting ditch dues. And if I try, I can imagine the secretary-treasurer poring over the accounts and deciphering the mayordomo's reports and filling out the account statements that will be dropped in the mail, hoping the numbers are right, that hours have been correctly translated into dollars and then divided or multiplied by the number of piones or shares or pesky fractions thereof.

A younger generation has taken over the running of the ditch, men in their forties and fifties. Now and then one of them calls or comes over and asks me about how things used to be done, how a particularly troublesome property got to be on the ditch when logically it should be irrigated from another ditch, about how the traditional water sharing agreement among the acequias during the dry months used to work (and not work), about the old days. For years there was a movement to "privatize" the March cleaning of the acequia, by having every parciante be responsible for the section of the acequia that flowed through his or her property. Then, at the customary ditch-cleaning time, a small crew would come through and dig out those sections of the ditch either not attached to a specific property or those the landowner had not got around to cutting back the brush on or digging out. The object of this change was to reduce the cost of the annual cleaning.

Last year after the new system had finally proven unworkable, the membership agreed to go back to the old way. The old way is to assemble a crew of twenty to thirty workers and start at one end of the ditch and cut back brush and dig out silt and gravel until the job is all done, after a day or two or three. I was pleased. *La Limpia, la saca*, the annual ditch digging, is probably one of the few exercises of communal labor still practiced in the nation.

Although I'm only a parciante now, the annual meeting remains an essential exercise in neighborhood democracy and consensus. I haven't missed more than one in thirty years. The ritual seems to vary little from year to year. In fact the meeting we hold in 2002 might differ little from that held in 1802, other than the language in which the proceedings are conducted. There are the young members, wanting to try something new every year. Well, I was one of them once. There are the old ones who say, If it isn't broken don't try to fix it. Now I guess I'm one of *them*. The same old ideas about how to deal with leaks, non-paying members, and water hogs are heatedly discussed, or not discussed, depending on whether those with leaky headgates or those who have not paid their ditch dues or those who hog water are present or not, often reaching crescendos of disapproval. Eventually the more sober realization sets in that punishing or fining or browbeating one's neighbors remains as problematical as ever. Particularly if they persist in not coming to ditch meetings. Finally we agree that we all have to work together, and the commissioners and mayordomo reluctantly consent to serve another term—"Well, if nobody else wants to do it." Meeting adjourned.

Most things haven't changed, but a few do. Throughout northern New Mexico there is a cadre of acequia activists working through organizations such as Community and Indian Legal Services of New Mexico, the Taos Valley Acequia Association, and the New Mexico Acequia Association. The latter has been instrumental in encouraging the formation of local watershed groups in order to better position acequias and the parciantes for present and future legal battles over water. There is now even an Embudo Valley Acequia Association which draws representatives from each of the ten acequias in and immediately below the valley. These efforts have already given the 1000 acequias of New Mexico a much stronger voice in the Legislature and the State Engineer Office.

Then there is what seems to hardly change at all, the actual acequia, the physical ditch channel, at least within the past thirty years. Here and there backhoes, even small bulldozers, have been brought in to re-dig overgrown sections whose banks have been prone to collapse into the fields below. But after a few years, willows return as vigorous as ever, and eventually cottonwood suckers will explore their way back into treeless sections. As ever, the ditch's rounded meandering banks, overgrown with vegetation, half-natural, half-manmade, remain a strangely beautiful creation, like something heaped and pushed into shape by giant gophers.

Here our 1802 time traveler might be confused—by the sight of the long files of willows and cottonwoods lining the ditch banks, and at the near absence of grazing animals which in the old days kept the banks clean. He would probably conclude that the acequia had been finally neglected beyond repair. He might even mutter what has surely been said at every acequia meeting since the beginning of time:

"The young ones, they don't know how to work. They don't know how to dig. Not like us, not like when we were young."

So turns the wheel of time.

|2001| Lazy, slow, clear, a stream meanders back and forth across a barren course of rocks and small boulders, from shallow pool to shallow pool, shadowed by willows and cottonwoods at the bends. Swallowtails, monarchs, painted ladies flit across the bright expanse and alight in the silvery green willows. Flycatchers work close to the water in quick bounds between low branches. The occasional cliff swallow races up the creek bed.

In the water tumbling over small boulders, soft greenish and blackish pods adhere to the rocks on the protected lower sides, while on the upper sides tiny larvae, black and stringy, cling jiggling to the rocks as the water rushes over them. Inch-long trout fry jerk through the warm eddies along the shore. On damp sand, over boulders, through grasses, ants and spiders scavenge, inspect, hunt.

This is the river in summer, my cooling refuge in the heat of the afternoon. At least for the most part. The exceptions being when it becomes a passionate creature, unpredictable, even dangerous, particularly in August and September. That's when surges of moisture from Gulf Coast hurricanes and from the Pacific Coast of Mexico collide with cool dry air over the Sangre de Cristo Range to generate what has come to be known as northern New Mexico's "monsoon" season—though the phenomenon is far more sporadic and unpredictable than the true monsoons of southern Asia. In its early, mild stages, giant anvil clouds build up over the mountains, producing mountain showers while teasing residents of lower altitudes with thin curtains of rain that evaporate before hitting the ground.

Later in the summer, heavy afternoon and early evening

downpours lasting an hour or more can strike the dry earth forcefully enough to seal it, sending rivulets of clay- and silt-laden water down slopes and into arroyos, picking up carpets of piñon and juniper needles and dead branches and old tires and trash along the way, snowballing into a foaming, odoriferous, muddy brown roll of water churning down toward the river. Within minutes a clear trout stream can be transformed into a roaring dark swath that will sweep away riverbank brush and logs and flatten willows and cottonwood saplings and suffocate fish and radically rearrange the architecture of the river bed.

Normally dry but capable of handling vast volumes of water, the arroyos that all feed into the river serve as instant tributaries and natural storm drains. And since the late summer storms tend to dump on isolated areas, in what sometimes seems like a daily rotation among Santa Fe, Los Alamos, Española, and Taos, it is relatively rare that the arroyos of northern New Mexico all run at once. If we happen to be driving home from Taos or Santa Fe during or after a downpour, the arroyos that are in flood will tell us which foothill areas have received the rain this time.

Once within the Embudo Valley, we must ford three arroyos within as many miles in order to get home: the Arroyo la Mina, Arroyo Pino, Cañada de Apodaca. On a few occasions we have had to wait for a half an hour for the water to subside before we could drive across. Twice at night we have had to park the car and wade across in order to get home. To the east, our dirt road dips down into the Arroyo de Apodaca before it joins the highway. I have often brought the tractor up and bladed the road back into shape after a flood along with other tractoring neighbors, sometimes before dawn in order to drive to the farmers' market.

After a really good storm, when the rain has stopped, but the arroyos are still raging, small crowds gather to watch the roaring waters and exchange rumors about which arroyos are still impassible, inspect the damage to the dips where the roads ford the arroyos, and follow the work of the highway department cranes fishing logs and stumps that have blocked the poorly designed galleries of the highway bridge. These landscape-transforming gully-washers excite in the same way as a thick blanket of winter snow: suddenly everything is different.

First to attempt crossing a still flooding arroyo are the more daring or foolhardy owners of high-suspension four-wheel-drive pickups and

SUVs, followed by ordinary pickups and older, higher cars, and lastly by the new and the shiny and the low-slung.

The intense late summer storms are a constant worry for acequia mayordomos who must weigh whether to shut down the ditch in advance of a storm that may dump its rains on the next valley over or wait until the arroyos start running and then risk being struck by lightning while tramping down to shut off headgates. During the worst downpours, such as one in the early 1970s which dumped four inches of rain on the valley in an hour, countless smaller arroyos and gullies send streams of water down the slopes and into the acequias, silting up and blocking the channels. The then-unfamiliar September storms terrorized us in 1971 when we were laying up the adobe walls of our house.

Once, while we were picnicking under clear blue skies in the mountains above Taos, less than twenty miles away, parts of the Embudo Valley were pummeled and pulped by hail—including our fields. Another time, someone raced up the drive and warned us of a "wall of water" coming down the arroyo toward the river, where my cousin John Pohlmann was exercising on a sandbank. Though he believes I rescued him from a muddy fate, I have never seen the arroyo-swollen river rise so fast that it could be considered dangerous. The risk comes not with the first tongue of muddy water, but a little later when the flood has gained momentum and is filling the banks and beginning to loosen boulders deep underwater.

And once, Rose Mary drove home from Taos in a blinding downpour, just minutes before four or five rockslides cut off the Rio Grande Gorge highway and a huge hole was gouged out of pavement when a boulder the size of garage tumbled two hundred feet down the canyon wall into the river. Though a number of cars were marooned between the slides, remarkably no one was injured.

And in September 1988, while on a visit to New York City, we picked up the *Times* and were startled to come across a front-page article about an accident in the Rio Grande Gorge four miles from where we live. During a severe thunderstorm late at night, a boulder the size of an office desk went through the windshield of a Greyhound bus, killing the driver and three passengers.

These storms can stop as abruptly as they start, and the hiss of rain is replaced with the sound of single drops falling from leaves and the distant roar of the swollen river and the smells of damp earth and vegetation. Within an hour or two, the river will have shrunken back to a stream again, its water tan with silt. Within a few days, it may be back to its former size, the water almost clear, though flowing through strands of sand and silt and past deposits of brown mud fringed with dark juniper and piñon needles and dry pine cones. As soon as the water lowers and the mud begins to dry, I inspect the river course for changes in the rocks and cuts into the banks and the fate of its borders of willows and grasses and watercress. If you get to the river early enough after a flash flood, you can sometimes find suffocated trout on the banks, still fresh enough to eat—which of course raises the question of the value of maintaining "in-stream flow" in order to protect aquatic habitat in those lower altitude sections of streams temporarily subject to devastating flash floods.

I have long wondered to what extent our floods are natural or the long term effects of logging and grazing. Alice Outwater, in her elegant study of the hydrology of North America, *Water,* suggests that the near-extirpation of beaver might be a cause. Their dams slow the flow of streams and redirect water into ponds and aquifers and impounded silt. Beaver, of course, were trapped nearly to extinction by the first Europeans and the Native American suppliers to the European fur trade. Prairie dogs also served to dampen the effects of downpours through their water absorbing burrows. They too have been systematically exterminated.

Within a couple of weeks, the river is back to normal and clear again. Gnats again hover over the water in the heat of the day. Eggs and larvae and even young minnow-sized trout begin to reappear. Grass and willows bent flat spring erect again. Other than the new layers of sand and mud, which quickly blend into the landscape, there will soon be few signs that the riverbed once contained a roaring flood. Here and there, four feet up in the crotch of a small tree or a clump of willows, there remain nests of twigs and leaves dropped by the receding waters—a reminder of how high the water reached.

When I lie down to dry on the new sand after taking a dip, I cannot help but keep an ear cocked for the next one. And wonder about the wisdom, in my former mayordomo days, of having driven all those beavers out of the acequia channel. . . .

III

CREATURES AND THEIR HABITATS

| 1995 | I live next to the border of two distinct worlds, one above the other.

The lower one I call home, a band of gently tilting bottom land that runs between hillside and river, in the narrow valley of a small tributary of the Rio Grande in northern New Mexico.

The other world looms right behind the house, just above the backyard. You can glimpse it through the three narrow slit-like windows we set in the north walls: the rocky, gravelly face of a two-hundred-foot-high bluff that rises above the lushness of the valley and to which cling yucca and small evergreens. "Piñon-Juniper Woodland" is the technical description of that other world, though the term "woodland" evokes something other than the reality, which is "Desert with Small Trees."

I do not go up there lightly or casually. The comparison may seem extreme, but the difference between the leafy lower riparian world and the hilly desert that hangs above is like that between shore and sea or earth and sky. And it is perhaps extreme to say that I find the piñon-juniper scrubland above a somewhat fearful place, a kind of Outer Space to where I make my home below, firmly in the valley. What has come to seem strange is how very close it is, only a few feet away, and how relatively rarely I step out the back door and bound up a dozen steps to the irrigation ditch, the acequia, and cross a plank bridge to the other side and begin ascending into that other world.

In fact it begins at the ditch itself, whose water artificially raises the wooded riparian zone a dozen feet up the side of the slope. This can be most readily seen from December until March when the acequia is dry. Step off the footbridge across the acequia and down into the channel, which is two feet deep and four to five feet wide, and you can see the change in the soil. On the down side, the fine silty clay of the ditch bank feeds a thick growth of willows, cottonwoods, wild plum, poison oak, innumerable grasses, hemlock, oshá (a wild borage), mint, alfalfa, and clover, depending on the sunlight hitting the bank as it winds this way and that—vegetation typical of the lower bottomland world, but maintained up here on a narrow shelf by the flow of the acequia from March until November. This bank, the south and lower, is made up of rich earth shoveled up out of the ditch channel year after year by the thirty-man spring-cleaning crew. The annual digging has been going on for hundreds of years under customs brought over from Spain in the seventeenth century. In most places along the three-mile acequia where the south bank is undisturbed by cattle or dogs or humans, these small annual additions in the form of shovelfuls of earth are serving imperceptibly to raise it higher. In some places the bank is nearly shoulder height in relation to the bottom of the ditch channel.

But turn now to the north and face the hillside. Within a foot or so of the ditch, the soil becomes sandy and rocky, bright and granular. In places where the acequia travels along a broad shelf of clay, it can feed a thick border of bottomland willows, but most stretches resemble the one behind our house, where the grasses become thinner and lighter in color, and squawberry and New Mexico olive and chamisa and yucca and small juniper and piñon trees, drought tolerant species all, replace the water-loving vegetation only a few feet downhill to the south.

Climb up out of the ditch to the north, or leap across it, and you immediately step away from the dappled and almost padded atmosphere of bottomland deciduous growth and begin ascending steeply into a world of sudden rockiness and aridity and glare. You can no longer go barefoot up here. You would do well to wear a hat. You might even think of carrying water. The hillside rises so steeply that you need to dig shoe or boot sideways into the loose gravel and sand to secure a foothold.

My only regular foraging now takes place in the fall when I cross the ditch with bushel basket and clippers in search of tender new juniper sprigs which Rose Mary weaves into wreaths; these are best cut from larger trees growing close enough to the ditch to tap into its water. Now and then we'll hike up to the top of the bluff, whose 6200-foot elevation is 200 feet above our house. We usually pick a warm winter or early spring day before the winds begin, sometimes to gather a small bag full of the segmented sticks of Mormon tea, and to survey the valley and its small adobe houses and mobile homes and orchards and gardens and fields spread out below, including the three fields that make up our small garlic farm. From the crest we marvel at how easy it is to distance ourselves from those thickets of relationship and worry and contention that lie spread out below, made miniature and oddly harmless by distance.

The stones for the foundation of our house came from the desert-like arroyos that finger their way up into these hills, and the volcanic black basalt blocks for the small circular building we call the tower, my first writing studio, were gathered from a hillside to the west with an ancient 1947 Chevy one-ton flatbed with high seventeen-inch wheels. That was twenty-five years ago, in those youthful days of testing my strength and endurance, and when I ended the day feeling good at having moved yet more tons of this or that—and when it was still legal, or more or less legal, to forage for rocks and firewood on BLM land, or dig gravel and sand.

Half the excitement of those expeditions lay in leaving the domestic world of the bottomland valley for that more hostile other world where you could get stuck in the sand or high-centered on a rock in an arroyo, and where you risked encounters in every step with the cactus that carpets certain areas of the hillsides and mesas above, or with imagined diamondbacks (which I have yet to encounter), and where in the dark low shadows of the small trees you imagined but rarely saw the gleam of the eye of the coyote, the gray fox, the jackrabbit, the bobcat, perhaps even the mountain lion, observing your slow progress in the high summer sun, your glistening back, and twitching at the thunk of stones being heaped higher and higher on the bed of the old silver truck.

I once went up into these places with a sense of heightened expectation and sensual arousal, perhaps not much different from whatever it is that lures drinkers up into some barren place to vent and drown their rage at the controlling world below, or at their figments of it, and lovers seeking to escape all eyes except those of the sky and the hidden creatures. Up in the arroyos and on dirt tracks leading away from the highway, you find signs of these furtive visits in little pockets of trashy desperation, piles of beer bottles and cans, and the paper and plastic detritus of human intimacy which the dry air quickly renders odorless. We all know, those of us who live in northern New Mexico, that these are the places where bodies have been found, in the juniper-piñon woodlands on the outskirts of Taos and Santa Fe and Albuquerque, and once even above this little valley, in the dry hills to the northeast.

The village buries its dead in this other world, on sandy hillsides, at the edge of arroyos, amid cholla and prickly pear cactus and rocks and gravel and sand, in its four cemeteries, and not in the arable bottom lands where the living all once had to till the earth and tend the herds and flocks. At a funeral some years ago, during the walk to a graveside service in the cemetery up the arroyo behind the village store, we passed below the small mound-like hills that cluster along a portion of the south side of the valley, where piñon and juniper cling to their steep sides and narrow ridges. On top of a knoll, ignoring our passage on foot below, a deranged young man sat with his boom box turned up loud with mariachi music, which howled on through the entire graveside service and perhaps even well after we had all hurried back down the dirt road in search of the leafy coolness below.

This other country, I tend to forget that I live only a few yards away from it and that a short steep hike uphill will carry me deep, or high, into a landscape that is much more sky than earth, where shade is low and prickly and where the view is peeled back to too much glaring light and yet veiled and undulating in the fore- and middle-ground, and the low round shapes of thickly needled trees block the line of sight at every turn—except skyward.

There is something inexplicable about the random dumping of countless different types of rocks, gravel, sand, a mantle of river stone rubble and volcanic shards over deposits of reddish and whitish clay and silt, which are exposed along the edges of arroyos and bared in cliffs. What geological cataclysms could have dumped and scattered and poured all these unrelated bits and pieces over such great expanses? Inland sea, river flood, glacier, volcanic explosion all come to mind as the forces that might connect these seemingly unrelated scraps, perhaps singly, perhaps in concatenation. The shadeless glare renders stone and pebble gemlike. You become convinced that you will encounter a shape truly precious or extraordinary within a few steps, a cut stone or old coin or arrowhead or shard of pottery. Eyes become glued to the ground in expectant search—and to avoid brushing against the low cactus that congregate in little thickets almost everywhere. As your booted feet carefully tread upon the paradoxically soft and almost spongy ground, your eyes will pick out the droppings of jackrabbits, coyotes, deer, and glide to the rusty tin can under the tree, about which you fleetingly wonder when and who, or to the pointed stump of a juniper cut with an axe for a fencepost or firewood generations ago. In the soft powdery patches of sand there are fresh prints of coyote and rabbit and feral dogs, perhaps even a smudged boot print. Here and there along the top of the ridge that overlooks the valley you come across small circles of blackened stones where fires were built on bright moon nights.

The sparse biological economy of this world seems monotonous from a distance, but a walk across its fragile ground will reveal its austere richness and its patient tenacity that can wait out periods of rainlessness lasting months at a stretch. In rounded irregular clumps like pads, small grasses grow in patterns suggesting enlarged lichens on rocks, perhaps the raised edges of the clumps forming miniature ponds to catch the snow and rain whenever they finally do come. Other species of vegetation seem to need to be near the fold of an arroyo where water occasionally flows or near a depression where it briefly collects or on a slope where the full force of the sun is tempered: chamisa with its black lower branches and fine fragrant leaves of pale turquoise and fall yellow flowers, sage whose pungent scent blooms in the rain, Apache plume with its feathery blossoms and seeds; New Mexico olive, a tall shrub of pale greenish bark; and sprawling tangles of squawberry from whose small red berries a tea can be made; or Gambel oak, whose low brushy growth emerges from networks of roots that can be as old as 800 years and whose presence signals yet another border, that of mountain scrublands. Until very recently, I had never chanced to climb our hillside at that time in spring when the native penstemon was in bloom—pink blossoms rocketing straight out of a south facing slope of dry clay and gravel.

But even amid the sparseness, there are enough berries and nuts and grass to support a surprising diversity of wildlife. Space is the key. Where down below we all huddle together around water—humans, animals, vegetation—and live almost on top of each other within territories carefully marked and maintained, up there the small trees are spaced apart almost as if planted a certain distance from each other, and the territories are vast and relatively endless.

I am always pleased to come back home from that other world, down from the bluff, slipping and sliding down the gravelly, rocky slope, to leap across the irrigation ditch and tramp down the steps back into this small oasis of flowing water and lushness and shade and relative order. But even down here that other world impinges on all sides and reminds us of its vastness and power each time we look up to the sky to note a change in the weather or the light of the season or when the coyotes howl in the evening from the top of the bluff. Its hills are the low screens from which weather and light emerge on all sides except to the east, which is commanded by the dark snow-dabbed wall of the Sangre de Cristo Range, whose peaks more than double our altitude.

The dry bluffs and cliffs just above our leafy treetops daily remind us down below how much in this arid land we are the exception, the rarity, and of the aqueous luxury in which we live—and thinness and fragility of the silvery strand of water from which we all feed and drink.

The dry hills hold back, as if waiting for the moment in the remote future when they will flow again, and rumble and churn, and close in again on this exception with a deafening clatter of rock and gravel.

|2000| They go so much together, the two, that you can hardly pull them apart. Mention the one and the other tags along: piñon, juniper.

These non-identical twins are the principal inhabitants of the gravelly slopes and mesas that rise above our Embudo Valley bottomland fields in a leopard-spotted pattern of evenly placed dark spots. Close to the road, you can distinguish the two: Rocky Mountain juniper, with its upward reaching branches and, commonly, more brownish foliage; pinon, with its more rounded, clumpy form. Up close, foliage in hand, juniper's segmented and branched scale-like leaves and strong cedar fragrance contrast with the short bunches of needles of the piñon and its distinctive sweet pine scent. And there is no mistaking the juniper's wrinkled blue-red berries—technically cones—and shaggy reddish bark with piñons' miniature "pine cones" and undistinguished gray bark. Lesson complete.

But sooner or later everyone is struck by what an inhospitable landscape this seems for a forest, albeit a sparsely populated one whose trees rarely exceed twenty feet in height. How on earth do they manage?

Well, they manage just like we do by killing off or generally discouraging everything else that might grow around them or feed off of them. The resins of piñon and volatile terpenes of juniper in their leaves and branches and roots contain compounds that serve as natural herbicides to suppress competing plants in the neighborhood, and the waxiness of their leaves and needles retains moisture for those long hot and dry, or cold and dry, periods of drought which can go on for years. And in spring their wind-borne pollen has probably driven off more than a few would-be human residents from their territory.

Humans are not the only species who gather and store piñon nuts, which by weight are as protein-rich as beef. Clark's nutcrackers and Steller's jays do the same, along with piñon mice and chipmunks. If you have ever been puzzled at the flocks of blue piñon jays flying around in a frenzy of a hundred or more during October harvest time, consider that each one of those protein-crazed birds may have as many as sixty piñon nuts in its esophagus, most of which will be deposited in communal caches in the woodland for later use. Such caches, those of humans excepted, are part of the reproductive strategy of the piñon, on the theory—if trees have theories—that jays and mice and squirrels, like humans who have too many bank accounts, can't keep track of them all. One of the first pieces of New Mexico law—or lore—delivered to me in 1969, within days of our arrival, on our first piñon nut hunt above Talpa, was that if you found such a cache you were by law supposed to leave half of it behind. Is there a lawyer in the woods?

Here juniper diverges sharply from its twin. Instead of relying on flocks of maniacal, forgetful birds, it has made a deal with Townsend's solitaire, a robin-sized gray bird whose multi-valent digestive system can cope with the juniper berry's concentrated terpenes while letting the seeds pass through undamaged. Other individualists such as robins and gray foxes also feast on the berries.

Divergence continues in matters of firewood. Sparkless, slow burning, piñon is hard to surpass in the fireplace—to the eventual peril of its slow-growing forests. Its delightful fragrance comes from a compound also found in Zinfandel grapes, which suggests the kind of wine best sipped around the fireplace. And where the use of piñon wood is largely ephemeral, juniper is permanent or at least long term, in the form of fence posts where its resins defend against fungi above and below ground. As a firewood, juniper is as spectacular as piñon is sedate and dependable, its pockets of resin blasting out great sparks. Not the sort of wood you want to burn unless you have a tight fire screen and have curbed all tendencies to leave the Sunday *New York Times* lying around within ten feet of the flames.

Other than the occasional hike up the hill behind our house, I am not a regular inhabitant of the juniper-piñon woodlands of northern New Mexico. Or no more than any other New Mexican who habitually drives through them every day, unheedful of the sometimes teeming bursts of life within. In our early years, like all our neighbors, we drove our pickup up to the mesa south of the valley to gather up the leavings of a great BLM tree crusher, in their effort to convert the piñon-juniper woodland into grassland more suitable to grazing. Recent concerns over the depletion of the piñon-juniper woodlands in the Peñasco area have led us to stop burning the wood, either gathered or bought.

And it's been some time since the days when, just before Christmas, I used to climb the hill with the kids and a small pruning saw to filch the top two feet of a piñon for a Christmas tree. Twenty-seven years ago, on the last such excursion with our five-year-old son Adam, we reached the top of the steep bluff and peered over the crest into the eyes of an equally startled buck mule deer. It stared at us briefly before springing down into an arroyo. Tugging at my sleeve, Adam gasped: "A reindeer!"

No, not a reindeer. Yet across that seemingly barren ground, where piñon and juniper and birds and small mammals have evolved together to manage their hardscrabble ecosystem in ingenious ways, you have the sense that almost anything could spring forth in the hallucinatory glare of a bright noon day.

|2001| It may seem contradictory to love the species while mistrusting the individual, but that is how I feel about cottonwood trees. My distrust is not about how they grow, which is fast, but how they fall over, which is even faster.

We were able to buy our two acres of bosque floodplain in the Embudo Valley thirty years ago because of lingering memories in the family who sold us the place. Just beyond our driveway entrance, there once stood the gray, weathered stump of an enormous cottonwood tree, shrouded in an overgrowth of squawberry and New Mexico olive, at the edge of the dirt road. Until a road crew bulldozed it away not long ago, it had served as a natural *descanso* or memorial to mark the site where one of the Maes boys was killed by a falling branch two generations ago.

Elsewhere branches have continued to fall ever since. Summer downpours and attendant winds unfailingly wrench off limbs and blow whole trees across the road. One summer night, we had a party of friends over. Their cars filled the driveway turnaround. Sometime in the early morning hours after everyone had left, a huge cottonwood toppled over, felled by some kind of root rot. The tree would have totaled three or four cars. Another windless June morning I was quietly hoeing the garlic when a sound as loud as a pistol shot announced the cracking of a heavy limb, which crashed promptly to the ground—for no good reason at all, except perhaps the tree had pumped too much water too high, too fast, up above an inherently weak "V" crotch.

Cottonwoods are phreatophytes ("well plants"), dependent on the shallow water tables of floodplains both for sustenance and germination, along with willows and the invasive tamarisk. A green cottonwood log is virtually sodden with water, water-logged, and thus inordinately heavy, while a log that has thoroughly dried out is almost as light and punky as balsa wood. These wet-dry, light-heavy extremes may be reflective of the air (and thus oxygen) retention strategies which enable cottonwoods to survive up to two seasons in water-saturated soils. Wet cottonwood will not burn but simply smolder interminably, while dry cottonwood will burn hot, fast, and sparkless. In moderate use, the wood has a reputation for burning off creosote in flues, but in excess it is blamed for burning out fireboxes. The soft, punky wood is technically a hardwood—another paradox. In economic terms, the easily carved wood is used primarily by Northern New Mexico *santeros* and drum makers. Otherwise it is the poor man's firewood.

Sometimes, when the seasons seem awry and we haven't seen rain for months and the river is a rocky channel cradling the merest trickle, I reassure myself by looking at the cottonwoods and thinking, Well, they're still here: everything must be all right. Spring is definitively crowned by the delicate light green of their leafing out in April, and their explosions of cotton from the catkins of female trees, which are banned in some cities, are timed to the likely arrival of the May-June floods. Wafting down through the faint breezes of late spring and early summer, the large white motes give body to the air. The cotton-swaddled seeds must touch moisture within a few days of their floating release, although as a backup feature the trees also propagate themselves through runners that reach deep into my bottomland fields and anywhere else where the water table is high. Hillside springs far above the floodplain are inevitably marked by wind-established copses of cottonwoods.

Cottonwoods are also natural swamp coolers. I have stood beneath one on a hot July day and felt pin-pricks of mist alight on my skin. Surely one of the great follies of all time was the 1970s federal Phreatophyte Eradication Program, which proposed to clear-cut the Rio Grande bosque from Socorro to San Juan, in the interest of "saving" water for the reservoirs of southern New Mexico. Had it gone through, the program would have eliminated splendid galleries of Plains or broadleafed cottonwoods and their attendant bosque habitat—and incidentally turned the Rio Grande Valley into a desert bereft of its natural air conditioning system which runs, you might say, on the swamp-cooler model.

The Embudo Valley where I live is a transitional zone between broadleaf species, whose heart-shaped leaves resemble those of aspens and poplars, and higher altitude narrowleaf cottonwoods with willow-like leaves, which predominate along the river below the drive and along the acequia back of the house. Under the right conditions in autumn, which is to say a succession of mild frosts, both types of trees will turn to gold and orange slowly and unevenly, bestowing a variegated shimmering display of heart-stopping color up to the beginning of November.

But with autumn, the trees are not done, particularly the narrowleafs. Their curving bare branches, a lighter gray than the broadleafs, and almost white in the uppermost spurs of new growth, reach into the clear blue skies to catch the rich low light of early winter, animating the cold, still days with a graceful presence.

I worry less now about falling branches and trunks, given all the greater risks out there. And though we occasionally thin out cottonwoods overhanging the sheds or the house, I am more tolerant of their suckers exploring the back yard. Sooner or later, when they reach a certain size, I will have them cut down and bucked up for firewood. Their slightly acrid, musky smoke scents the living room, and in the fireplace they transform themselves into orange flames and heat, leaving finally a heap of fluffy white ash, which I will shovel up and spread out in the garden, resuming the cycle again.

| 1989 | Everybody needs a river.

The one I live beside is hardly that much of the time. It runs between being a river when at flood, muddy, noisy, deep, wide flowing, when you would not dare call it a stream, to being so dry in June or August that you would not call it a stream for the opposite reason. You would call it a ruin, a desert that bears signs of once having been a receptacle for flowing water. Yet I think of it as a river and flatter it by calling it such.

The river flows past where I live, past the bottom of our field, in an S bend marked by files of tall shaggy narrowleaf cottonwoods, whose trunks of light gray bark lean over the water as if to witness what endlessly passes there. Source and destination are in places visible: twenty miles to the east rises the sierra of the Sangre de Cristo Range, whose winter snows slowly translate into this water, and then whose summer rains; and a few miles to the west where the stream's cold and modest flow mingles with the warmer waters of the Rio Grande to join the long, fitful caravan toward the Gulf of Mexico.

Every day I walk down our dirt driveway to visit the river and give a quick glance at its steaming, icicle-festooned course in the low month of January, or a lingering evening farewell in the spring and summer and warm still dusk of early autumn. Rose Mary and I have raised children who have paddled and swum and fished from its banks. Every afternoon in summer we walk down to cool ourselves in its waters and lie on the tiny beaches of fine gray sand, down at the S bend, not far below our house, which is that part of the river I know best and is the stretch, a hundred yards or so, I consider most mine, most part of what I am.

Our beach is a bend, an elbow, a roll of sand and rocks and silt dropped by receding floodwaters over the years, and where willows and cottonwoods attempt to establish purchase, to turn it into a bank. Clover, alfalfa, jimson weed, squawberry, and even the odd clump of prickly pear cactus grow there too, to be often swept away or flattened by the brief summer floods. I never tired of meditating on the endless shapes and textures of rocks and pebbles that the aeons have mixed and dumped here, pieces of shale and granite, schist and basalt and quartz; and occasionally I have found a fossilized shell which serves to remind me that this small river is but a faint memory of an ancient sea. And along here, the water steps down musically across rocky shoals into a slow, quiet pool where its warmer surface flow joins chill subterranean waters before stepping down again, splashing and gurgling, to a lower string of pools, faster and clearer, where brown and rainbow trout pass their days in studied levitation.

The river gathers others. Muskrats work the shady, stiller pools. Water ouzels, whose out-of-water knee bends must serve to warm them up for their submersions, ply the whiter stretches. Experts in matters of flood, killdeer build austere nests on the higher sandbars strewn with the pebbles their eggs so cannily blend in with, and their plaintive alarms echo the length of the river from spring into summer. With long beaks and legs and white and tan markings, they are like small sea birds that have decided to try inland living for awhile, and not happily. I have found three nests in my time. The louder the parents' cries of alarm, the further from the nest they have succeeded in luring me; it is when this ever-restless couple grows quiet and stands still almost out of sight by the edge of the water that I know I am getting warm. Like water dribbling into sand, right in front of my feet, their chicks have vanished into thin air.

A kingfisher now and then cruises my stretch of the river. Cliff swallows race the open course between the trees, flying low just before it rains and invading the strata more usually claimed by the sleek and rarer barn swallows, with their clicking beaks. Bats pass the days in cool root-hung caves where the river has cut away into the bank; they come out at night and claim the lower sky, while nighthawks sieve the warmer air above of its insect life, an atmospheric plankton that has been kicked aloft by invisible streams of cool air rolling down from the high mountains at dusk.

And spring is announced by turkey vultures returning home to roost in the tops of the cottonwoods along the river. They ride back from Mexico each March on the storms that shuttle our water back from the Gulf and arrive one by one in the wind, the rain, even the snow, thirty or forty in the flock that has claimed this stretch of the river. Dark hulks in the treetops, after a wet night they will begin the morning by hanging out enormous wings to dry in the rising sun, while waiting for the first breezes to carry them aloft for a day of soaring over the valley in wide, wide circles, around the river, through the summer, until late September when, one by one, they will leave on the wings of the autumn storms, as they have done for generation after generation, perhaps for thousands of years.

A trip to the river was once a treat for a magpie we adopted as a windfall fledgling, and there it learned from us how to paddle and then sunbathe, ruffling its feathers and spreading out its wings and tail in the sun to dry. Once a gray Toulouse goose from our flock strayed down to the river in the spring in search of a secret place to nest. While bathing in the high flow and preening herself on the bank, perhaps she recovered some mythic dream or memory from the ancient times before the slavery of domestication. She ignored my cajolings to rejoin the flock and even the distant calls from her flock. Finally she went on her way downstream and disappeared. After all, everybody needs a river.

I carry the river around in that floating landscape of memories, images, and ideas that makes up one transitory human being, this "myself." As through the narrow mountain valley where I live, it runs through the center of my being. Cottonwoods line its length, gray clouds of overarching growth that open out into quaking mists of soft green, which then ripen into brief blazes of gold and then grow into gray traceries again over the course of a year. The waters below mirror the clear blue skies of winter, then grow muddy, recede, sparkle, then dull with the algaes of high summer, then gather up the bright falling leaves, then build sheets and stalactites of ice in the morning mists of winter.

I am but an aspect of the river, one of its points of consciousness. Even when not in its presence, I feel the river running, I measure its flows, I run my eyes over its stones and pebbles, I note the glint of its surface, the sound of its water rustling over stones and through the roots of its banks, its waters which connect to all skies, and to oceans everywhere.

|1996| "What do you use them for?" The visitor stands in the living room staring out the window at our flock of geese grazing on the lawn. He may be noting their full-breasted, deep-draft plumpness. "Do you eat them?"

No, we don't eat them, not even their remarkably large eggs. But yes, they're useful. They mow the lawn. They eat our kitchen scraps. They love lettuce and spinach and beets. On harvest days we dump into their pen buckets full of leaves and stems and bulbs culled out while washing and bunching and boxing our produce for the farmers' market. When a zucchini escapes our notice and balloons to gourd size, we lug it over to the goose pen. After the first frosts of autumn, we gather up all the immature and damaged winter squash and apples going soft for the geese. They're our feathered garbage disposals and composters.

We don't eat them. I suffer from the modern squeamishness about slaughtering—or the human sentimentality and arrogance that would place us on a higher and somehow exempt position, allowing us to eat without getting blood on our hands. I'm on slippery footing here. Yet the question, "Do you eat them?" rankles me in the way a pet owner would be offended by a similar question about his cats and dogs. Eat them? Is that all people can think about?

Yet they are not exactly pets. They lack the emotional dependency of dogs and cats. As a flock whose numbers vary from twelve to eighteen from year to year, they have their own customs and politics. They are companions of a sort, giving life to our domestic landscapes of lawn and orchard and field. Their chortlings and cacklings and honkings that break into conversations in the living room and echo through the neighborhood are among those sounds that tell us where we are.

As the gray flock waddles across the lawn, long necks bobbing almost in unison, beaks pointing in the same direction like a school of fish, my delight in them refreshes itself each time I pause in my own comings and goings to sit down and lose myself in their business of eating and preening and fighting and resting and dozing.

Geese, like most domesticated animals, don't mind being watched. They have learned how to put up with the intense human stare, which can so readily spook creatures in the wild. As a result, the flock has another kind of utility in its collective habits and individual quirks of personality, which is that it serves as a steady and ever-present lens, slightly distorting, into that which is so veiled and fleeting in the wild.

The flock is descended from a single pair of Toulouse geese my wife Rose Mary and I bought from an old Taos woman in the mid-1970s. At the time, most villages and small towns still featured a few characters who kept every kind of fowl they could find—chickens, ducks, guinea hens, geese, peacocks—along with rabbits, a few goats and sheep, perhaps even pigs and a cow, usually within a backyard of falling down fences, decrepit hutches, crumbling haystacks, leaning sheds and henhouses. These Noah's Arks, survivors of the floods of agricultural change, are much rarer than they used to be. Rose Mary and I launched one such ark for about ten years while our kids were growing up, finally dispersing most of its inmates when we decided we needed to get away from the place now and then for more than a day at a time.

We kept the geese. Toulouse geese are patient, low-maintenance birds with rich grey feathers and natty white rumps and carrot-orange beaks and feet. They lack the beak hump of the smaller white Chinese geese (or so-called grey African), which are singularly restless and chattery. Their hyperactive manner makes them ideal for weeding cotton fields and other non-edible crops.

Our pair of Toulouse geese grew to a flock of fifteen birds over the course of several years. Geese mate in late winter, a public business lasting thirty seconds to a minute. The ponderous mounting of gander onto goose followed shortly by a crooning orgasmic tumble back off elicits much public comment and apparent criticism by the onlooking flock, who will often drive the coupling pair apart. Soon after the hen scouts out nesting sites in fenceline hedges inside and outside the pen, most often returning to a previous nest site. Seated on the ruins of an earlier nest, the hen extends her long neck out and picks up twigs and straw with her beak and draws them into a circle around her, completing the work by plucking down from her underbelly. This is the occasional work of about two weeks.

From this point forward, our rather elderly flock now suffers all kinds of problems. Hens often claim the same nest and upset the delicate schedule of incubation, during which eggs must be regularly turned and dampened down with water shaken off the hen's recently bathed feathers. Visits away from the nest for quick bites of grain, a drink and a dip in the water tub must all be prepared for by covering the eggs with a blanket of down. Nesting geese are not easily spooked if they are approached and worked around slowly, but a lunge by a passing dog or a sudden turn of the tractor on the other side of the hedge or even an attack by a jealous rival will send a goose off the nest in a panic, leaving the eggs exposed to the cooling air.

The thirty-five-day incubation cycle, which starts after the laying of as many as fifteen eggs, reduces the hen to a smelly sack of feathers and bones, with beak and feet nearly drained of color. Then begins the complicated business of hatching the young and launching them out into the world. Mishaps abound. Goslings hatch over a period of two or three days. By the end of the hatching period the first goslings out are restless and hungry and the last barely strong enough to walk.

We ready the cardboard box, the 15-watt light bulb, the towel, and the mayonnaise jar lid for water. Every year there seems to be at least one orphan. We call them all Gulliver. One year a cloudburst with hailstones so weakened a gosling that we had to bring him inside. A king snake nearly strangled another. Several have found themselves unable to get out of the shallow water tub. Others have got caught in thickets of brush. Then there are the usual familial misunderstandings. Two hens can make claims on a gosling, confusing its imprinting mechanism. For this and other reasons, a gosling can find itself excluded from the warmth of down-lined feathered skirts as darkness falls.

Geese are not compassionate in any human sense. The weakened or diseased or motherless gosling is chortled over briefly and then left to fend for itself. Sooner or later it falls over and ends up on its back, legs peddling in the air, peeping weakly. That's when I put on gloves and boots and step inside the pen.

Geese are ferociously protective of their young. Even after twenty years of dealing with them, I do not lightly enter the pen to rescue a gosling in distress, knowing that whatever my muttered apologies and explanations I will be greeted with lowered necks, hissing beaks, and wings raised high and outspread. No matter that the flock has apparently disowned the helpless gosling. The moment I bend down to pick up the peeping waif, I know the mother goose will lunge at me with beating wings and clamping beak.

Newly hatched goslings are famous for bonding or imprinting with whoever or whatever becomes their keeper. This is all very endearing. The gosling, affection at first divided between the light bulb in the box and the large human head that regularly appears over the top and hands that offer snippets of grass and scraps of lettuce, soon peeps plaintively at your slightest movement.

But you can't simply keep a gosling in a box. It needs exercise, it needs to learn how to graze on the lawn, how to swim, it needs to become strong enough to get out of the water or out of thickets of grass, holes, and ditches. And it needs to do these things with you near and watching. But how flattering to have a gosling follow you around the house and garden, snuggling up to ankle and dropping off to sleep or twittering lightly in cupped hands.

Rose Mary and I have trained countless Gullivers. A number have been too weak to bring around and have quietly slipped back into the elements. Many have recuperated without fully bonding to us and have re-entered the flock. Some of those have survived marauding magpies and snakes and probably even coyotes and foxes and owls and have reached adulthood. Many others that we rescued very young became so firmly bonded to us that we couldn't release them to the flock until they were strong enough to fend for themselves if rejected by one or another prospective mother.

We learned quickly that if you take a human-imprinted gosling up to the fence and set it down and walk away, it will follow you back to the house over the protests of the flock. Eventually we devised a method to de-imprint a gosling of our presence and re-imprint it with a goose hen or with the flock in general.

The method is simple. I first let out the flock and herd it around to the back of the house. Then I go inside. Eventually the geese graze their way back around the house toward their pen, which I can observe out the west living room window. Just before they clear the southwest corner and fan out on to the lawn, I slip out the front door with Gulliver and release him in the grass, then dash back inside. With other goslings in tow, the flock comes across the plaintively peeping waif. They surround him. Obvious conclusions are drawn. He looks like one of ours, the geese chortle to each other. He probably *is* one of ours. This must be one of our long-lost offspring. . . .

Gulliver undergoes a similar if less certain and less immediate conversion. There is something oddly familiar about these creatures, he must be thinking. They seem to talk my language. Eye contact is far easier. Could these be my long lost parents and siblings. . . ?

Grazing resumes. Gulliver uncertainly joins his siblings, now and then looking up and peeping. Mother goose chortles reassuringly while pulling at the grass, as if to say, This is how you do it. For a time he stays a little apart from his fellows, but by the end of the day he's indistinguishable.

Geese take two years to assume their adult personalities. For the first few months they are more stomach than brain, fuzzy camouflage-green eating machines that tear at the lawn all day long and squirtingly defecate every few minutes. By late summer they have grown into gangly, panic-prone adolescents, still not awakened from the endless eating dream. By the end of summer they are fully fledged and nearly adult in size, ready for what would be their first migratory flight in a state of nature—yet still clumsy and brainless, often becoming confused about how to get through the open gate for their afternoon sessions on the lawn or back inside the very same open gate at nightfall. In flight, could they fly, their trembling eyes would be fixed on beacons of whiteness ahead, the rumps of the leading elders who know the way, and on their companions' beaks, bright orange running lamps, to either side.

Our visitor turns away from the living room window. So if we don't eat them, he may be musing, then we don't know what they taste like. Roast goose has a festive ring to it—especially now that we're all so weary of turkey. "I understand they're wonderful watchdogs," he ventures in the hope of moving the conversation to more certain ground.

Perhaps he entertains visions of thieves running down the drive, throwing TVs and microwaves into the bushes, as pursued by a flock of hissing, honking geese. I know of only one such act of heroism. It took place during the Second World War. An older acquaintance of mine marched through France and Germany as an infantryman without firing his rifle until he stepped into a Bavarian farmyard where he was attacked by a goose. He shot the defender of the household dead.

"Watchdogs? Actually not," I reply. "They make lousy watchdogs. Though I'm pleased that people think otherwise." I hope the word has spread throughout the underworld to stay away from houses guarded by geese.

Geese are aggressive only during the nesting and rearing season from late spring until early fall, though they can be trained to be "mean" all the time—as any creature can. For the most part they will not go out of their way to make a run at a dog or child or an adult who keeps out of the territorial circle of pen or grazing pasture and who steers clear of their young. A car coming up the drive or a stranger approaching the front door will elicit none of the hollering that greets a familiar figure at feeding time. But if I approach in the company of another human, stranger or not, they will huddle together and grow silent. They know from experience that if there is more than one of my kind I am likely to climb into the pen to corner a goose and seize it by the wings at the shoulder joint and lift it up and lower it into a burlap sack or cardboard box, where it will tremble in terror. Then follows the incomprehensible drive in the trunk of a car or the back of a pickup to another pen, a sordid version of the once stately migrations. After such an incident, my geese are silent for a day or two whenever they see me, but soon they're back to nagging me to feed them or let them out of their pen to graze on the lawn every time I step out the front door.

I offer my visitor a seat. He steps away from the window and slumps down on the couch. We begin the conversation that has brought him here. Something about water or farming. It is early spring, a good time for such conversations, just before the real work begins. Suddenly outside there is a great ruckus of beating wings and angry honkings. My visitor jumps to his feet. "A couple of geese are trying to kill each other," he exclaims.

Well, no, not exactly, I suggest. It may look like that, a fight to the death, but it's just a ritual in which two ganders work at maintaining or recasting the pecking order. The outcome has some bearing on the more or less monogamous mating relationships within the flock.

The fights begin with the ganders throwing necks over each others' shoulders and grabbing hold of back feathers with beaks in order to lock themselves together chest to chest. Thus engaged, they beat at each other with their long wings, which span six feet tip to tip, pushing against each other with their feet. It's as if two men embraced and boxed each other with elbows. The damage caused by this noisy, flapping contest is negligible. The flock gathers around the boxers and cheers them on. The fights last a minute or two at the most, until one of the ganders loses his balance and falls over and runs away. Beak lowered, neck arched, wings raised, the victor briefly chases the loser and then struts, honking in triumph. The kibitzing flock lets forth with a concluding chorus of full-bodied honkings. Then everybody, including the winner and loser, go back to the essential business of grazing the lawn.

This raucous business is likely to erupt at any hour of the day or moonlit night from late January until April. At night you can easily imagine a coyote in the pen lunging at the flock. But the reality is that geese are relatively quiet when under attack. They signal an emergency by little more than beating wings and faint strangled cries. Some years back a large owl was making raids on the flock, which I discovered only because a duck hen in a neighboring pen called out a quacking alarm at four in the morning.

Ducks, in short, make better watchdogs. Or dogs, for that matter.

The best time to observe the workings of the flock is when I have let them out of their pen on to the lawn and apple orchard, where they can be viewed from the south living room window or from lawn chairs outside. The flock first fans out across the grass. The geese settle into a loose formation at about ten feet apart. Either a senior goose hen, not a gander, or a goose more active than the others leads the flock toward a preferred patch of grass or a long-remembered planting of lettuce or carrots in the garden. From a distance sometimes, but not always, I can guide them away from a forbidden destination with a loud hiss.

The alpha gander presides over all with an observant, upright, beak-tilted-into-the-air attitude. He seems to eat little. Periodically he issues a grunt-like honk. Abruptly he runs at another gander, jabbing him in the rump or side. The victim springs away, ruffles feathers, resumes foraging. By these minor attacks the gander asserts his alpha status, as do the lesser ganders all down the pecking order. Nature seems to be saying that power is best exercised through arbitrary actions.

The alpha gander also sounds the alarm. This quickly brings together the flock in a drill in which it runs from one end of the lawn to the other, wings flapping, honking, necks lowered, either to the apple trees at the south end or the adobe house at the north, where they come to a halt on strutting tiptoes. In nature, with birds not fattened by corn and lazy from confinement, the drill would result in flight. At best, in a down-hill run toward the orchard with a brisk side-wind from the west, the flock can become momentarily airborne, a few inches off the ground. The attempt concludes with wings extended and flapped once or twice to straighten feathers before being folded back up. Then there is a brief necks-lowered conference during which no one seems to be blamed for this daily collective failure to attain their ancient freedom. Feathers are preened. Foraging resumes.

From April to November, I flood the lawn every week or so with water from the acequia up behind the house. Geese are adaptable creatures; they can live their lives on land, on awkward feet and weak legs, with nothing more than a basin of drinking water. But when water gushes through their pen and flows across the lawn, they regain their paradise of river and lake lost through domestication and confinement, and they become free and playful again. They seek out ditches and holes to sit and root around in, dipping their necks and throwing water on their backs, ruffling feathers and preening themselves. A depression or hole in the turf is an invitation to create a small pond by tramping up and down in one place and then pulling out loosened grass and roots. With great abandon they throw their necks onto their backs and roll them back and forth, eyes closed, beaks ajar. All become lost in their separate worlds of water, grass, and sun.

At least until one of them makes a signal. I haven't yet managed to observe who makes it or what exactly it is. In a wink the flock scrambles, runs around in circles honking and flapping wings in a madcap frolic. Just as abruptly it all ceases. The flock gathers together, lowers necks, chortles for a moment, then resumes grazing.

■

The geese are all individuals. Two are marked by deformities, a broken wing and a growth on a beak. The old gander, father of them all, was always a stern and easily recognizable presence, as was the mother goose with her self-effacing, searching ways. Some years ago a young gander began calling attention to himself by waddling over to the fence and greeting me, wanting to engage in dialogue—or so I imagined. The other fifteen geese would stand their distance and warily inspect my gestures or even run at the fence during nesting season.

But not this one. He would approach, chortling, head lowered, and nibble like a parrot at whatever was within reach, while casting shy upward glances. After I tossed the flock their ration of grain and kitchen scraps and returned to the house, I imagined him rejoining his peers to offer some interpretation of my human behavior, my moods, and speculations on my dark and confusing plans. I came to think of him as the Ambassador Gander.

He was somehow different from his fellows. There was something in the cast of his eyes and the way he held his head that reminded me of a young friend I had not seen in years. A slightly in-turned foot gave him a slower, more waddling walk. He became the regular loser in the ganders' ritual fights, which meant he could never keep a mate. In time it became apparent that he was not quite part of the flock. He remained always a little separate yet healthy enough to defend himself against the random persecutions that seem a feature of any flock in captivity.

With age, he developed arthritis in his knees, at about the same time his father or grandfather did, the grand Old Gander whose decline stretched over the better part of a spring, summer, and autumn. Eventually the Old Gander became so lame he was unable to walk. Yet the flock still respected the pecking order. Neither the next gander in line nor any of the junior ganders tried to beat up the Old Gander or drive him into the bushes.

In nature the sick and dying, the injured, the deformed, are all liabilities to the flock, the herd, the school. In confinement the sick chicken or duck or goose is commonly pecked and hounded and driven from food and water, even cannibalized in the case of chickens, behavior that strikes humans as cruel, even when the rationale is clear. But the true cruelty lies in the initial confinement by humans, which converts a functional ostracism into a grisly form of persecution.

The Old Gander was left alone. I made sure he had food and water within reach, under the shade of an apple tree. He died the first week in a November twenty years after we had brought him down from Taos with his mate. He could have been as much as twenty-five years old.

The Ambassador Gander was not so lucky. As he aged and found it harder to walk, he was more and more tormented by the other ganders. Before I realized how desperate matters had become, the flock blinded him in one eye. I realized my mistake. No Ambassador Gander at all, he was at the very bottom of the male pecking order. My friend, the Omega Gander. The pariah. All those years he had been appealing to me to be rescued from his kind.

I separated him from the others. We worked out a routine where he'd come to the gate during the morning feeding, and I'd let him out alone on the lawn where he would spend the rest of the day. Lame with swollen joints, he never strayed far. The vegetable garden lay well beyond his browsing range. Late in the afternoon when I let out the flock, he would keep his distance until dark, when I would coax him back inside the pen after the others. He spent the night in brush-clogged hedges, safe from the enemies of his own kind and from the four-legged creatures that prowl through our two acres at night: dogs, coyotes, foxes, bobcats, skunks, and weasels.

Lawn privileges didn't earn him any points with the others. On occasion he tried to adopt a Gulliver who still harbored uncertainties about his parentage. His last year he developed a crush on an old goose, until a sure-footed rival took her away. I had hoped his grassy diet might gain him some relief from his arthritis, possibly the effect of confinement in an unnaturally non-aquatic environment. Once a visiting child who had a way with animals walked right up to him on the lawn, stooped down, and embraced him. For an instant the two knew the joy—and terror—of interspecies kinship.

One spring he died inside the pen, sometime in the night or early morning. He was close to twenty years of age.

I have been harsh on my hypothetical composite visitor. Though I have never slaughtered or eaten any of our geese, I do now and then think of them as an emergency reserve—but one I hope I'll never have to tap into. They embody a couple of hundred pounds of protein and fat, with much left over in bones and gristle for the dogs and cats, and perhaps a down comforter or two. These are not entirely idle thoughts. Not in these days when most cities live with only a three-day reserve of foodstuffs on hand.

But I don't usually think of them as a form of basic insurance. More important, they are part of what I am as a human being. As domestic animals become more and more absent as common features of everyday life, except as shrink-wrapped frozen meats, there is cause to be concerned about what we are inflicting on animals by converting them into scarcely living creatures confined to animal factories as well as what, indirectly, we are doing to ourselves.

In emptying our backyards and turning livestock production over to the corporations, we are cutting one more link to our collective past and to the natural world itself. At the lowest level, our domesticated species provide an escape route back toward earth-connected and less centralized livelihoods. This is not a romantic or Luddite concern in an industrial world whose unsustainable practices are on a headlong collision course with the realities of Nature.

A family with a flock of geese or a few chickens and a garden is by no small measure more independent of global systems of production and distribution than a family that must shop as a condition for meeting every human need, as prompted by the magic show of our time.

My geese remind me that historically I have been herder and hunter both, and that some day those skills may have to be reclaimed, that they may become more important than knowing how to drive a car or use a computer. It seems improbable enough now, but will I some day have to teach a grandchild or great-grandchild how to herd a flock of geese? Will I have to explain that it's much like pouring water from a bucket into a jar? That you aim with the tip of the flow?

And what of them, the geese? Do they look on me as someone who has used his superior intelligence and power, his opposable thumbs that have mastered the use of metals, to force them into confinement? Or do they think—as I sometimes think of my own society—that this can't go on and that sooner or later I will lose my touch? Do they hope that some day the fences will finally sag and the gates drop from their hinges and that there will be nothing blocking their way down to the river, which they hear in the distance through the night?

But we're in this together. My geese, descendants of the European greylag geese studied by Conrad Lorenz, can no more return to the wild than I can, in this alien continent. We're dependent on each other. We're locked together in civilization. Release them to the wild, to the river at the bottom of the drive—where a goose escaped several years ago, to a brief life of watery freedom, now and then calling back to the flock from its Outer Space through the screening cottonwood trees, until the flock's answering honkings were finally met with silence— release them to the wild, and they won't make it for long.

Release me from civilization? I wouldn't make it, not alone, not without them, not without countless other creatures we have collectively coaxed and dragged and lured into our common protective enclosure.

| 1996 | The gourd people are a strange lot.

They call several times a year. They need gourds of a certain size. They need a dozen or two for a school project. They need them quickly and want them cheaply. Could they drop by this afternoon on the way to Taos or Santa Fe?

What is strange here is not the nature of the request, which is ordinary enough, but the urgency with which it is usually made, suggesting that the caller not only needs gourds but is also desperate to talk about them.

But as a gourd person, I am equally quirky. I give several types of evasive answers. "Well, I haven't really sorted my gourds yet." Or, "I want to keep them all because I like to have a two-year supply on hand in case of a crop failure." I am careful not to admit that I may well have a five- or ten-year supply on hand, a thought that makes me very happy indeed. I even suggest, "They're easy to grow, why don't you plant some yourself?" I hope my caller doesn't detect the fallacy here: if they're so easy to grow, why do I keep a two-year or five-year supply on hand? We are very strange, us gourd people.

I invariably refer gourd people to the newsletter of the American Gourd Society of Mt. Gilead, Ohio. It has the easy-to-remember title "The Gourd." I am a faithful subscriber. Subscription gets you a membership card in the American Gourd Society but no frequent flyer miles, rental car discounts, or sweepstakes opportunities. Once or twice I have flashed my card at incredulous non-gourd persons, to disappointing effect. The card lacks the hologram and magnetic strip of true financial power.

Gourds fall into two types: small ornamental gourds of the sort you find in supermarkets in November sporting an improper coat of urethane or some other toxic varnish; and hard-shell Lagenaria ("large flask") gourds.

Ornamental gourds, the name suggests, have no use. They are small and their shells are thin. Skins hold their orange and green stripes and white blotches for a few months at best. They grow into shapes resembling 3-D spoons, pears, balls, eggs, lumpy pears, lumpy balls, lumpy eggs, and one called "crown of thorns," which evokes the bud of a giant flower badly rendered in plaster of paris.

Useless as they seem to be, we have managed to use them, or use them up, in various ways. Rose Mary dyes the small spoon gourds in Rit dye, stinking up the kitchen, and ties them with waxed twine to garlic arrangements. I drill or poke the gourds whose shape she doesn't like and string them on baling wire in three-foot lengths. When fresh, the strings can make a pretty display in the greenhouse where I hang them to dry, which helps the gourds retain a blush of orange and yellow, with no mold spots. I also tie small gourds on a length of waxed twine so they dangle below my hard-shell-gourd bird feeders. Use? To use up spoon gourds.

I used to grow ornamental gourds an acre at a time. Once I took a painter friend over to the field to take a look. She was entranced. As we all looked down into the tangle of vines shading the small shapes, she murmured, "Like sea shells on the beach."

A field of gourds bestows on you a sense of natural wealth like nothing else. With all this at your command, how could you not become a millionaire? Well of course you already are one: a gourd millionaire. I have regularly imagined a Gourd Factory that would turn them all into I'm not certain what, but whatever it was to be there would be a lot of it. The reverie fades when you try to translate your tens of thousands of gourds into nickels and dimes and quarters and dollars, which is when you begin to discover that you might be gourd poor. This becomes even clearer during the stoop labor of gathering them up in the field in the cruel penetrating light of October and figuring out how to string and dry them before they freeze and become moldy.

Useless? No, not quite. A dried ornamental gourd, light as a feather, is a fine toy for a baby not yet strong enough to smash the thing into bits. The two-year-old, in that harmless and gratifying gesture, will expose a bolus of shredded-wheat-like material in which are suspended dozens of small squash-like seeds.

Luffas are of the ornamental gourd family. Their internal shredded wheat material is commonly used as scrubbers. I grew some one year, entertaining visions of retooling the Gourd Factory so that I could become the Luffa King of the Southern Rockies. But the idea, like so many gourd ideas, fizzled. I had no wish to make use of such a thing myself, either in the bathtub or in the dishpan. For the latter, I much prefer those curly plastic pot scrubber balls.

They last forever.

Hard-shell gourds are for the serious gourd people. You see the elite in the grainy black and white photos of "The Gourd" as they stand beside their displays of gourd pots, gourd hats, gourd planters, gourd birdhouses, gourds tortured into bizarre shapes, and as they pose next to their backyard trellises from which dangle dipper gourds with thin straight necks four feet long.

The smallest hard-shell gourds, rattle sized, will be no larger than an ornamental gourd. The largest barrel gourds can grow to a diameter of two feet. Growing season is a limiting factor where I live. The best I can produce is a bottle gourd eighteen inches tall and ten inches in diameter, in the shape of a squat bowling pin. Birdhouse gourds have a thin, tapering neck, and the longer necks of dipper gourds, if not trellised, will curl this way and that. The so-called caveman's club is a long, tapered cylinder, usually with a fragile shell. Barrel gourds are spherical, not barrel shaped, and tobacco pouch gourds are the size of a large buttercup squash, in a round and flattened shape. Before they dry out, all hard-shell gourds are a light to dark green, sometimes spattered with whitish blotches. They cure to tan, sometimes by way of a dark brown stage triggered by frost, which is very smelly, as in: "There's something dead in the room." This smell will return under certain kinds of heat, even when the gourd is dry. While preparing to retool the Gourd Factory to produce my latest innovation, I festooned the living room with hanging gourd lamps. Several weeks into the new lighting, we finally pinpointed the deathly odor that emerged halfway through our evening newspaper reading as emanating from the gourd shades.

What distinguishes hard-shell gourds from their ornamental cousins is revealed in the name: their hard shells. Or more or less hard. Hardness of a peculiar kind, being in part a function of their rounded shape, which is where their true strength lies, combined with the almost fragile brittleness of the shell, which can be as thin as a sixteenth of an inch in a just barely cured gourd or as thick as a quarter inch in a fully matured and prosperous one. But even a strong gourd can be easily shattered with a hammer or a foot; and the tip of a knife blade, firmly applied, can readily penetrate the thickest of shells. The shell material is roughly as strong as piece of pine or spruce of the same thickness, though it has no pronounced grain.

A gourd's rounded shape invites it to be carried off somewhere else, for some other use, by the human hand. The wind can even nudge a gourd some distance once its tethering vines have withered away. It floats, of course, at least for awhile, until enough water to sink it leaks into its navel, that point where the calyx dropped off; but the leaky spot can easily be smeared with pitch or wax to enable the shell to float indefinitely.

A gourd is a top-of-the-line seed case. Inside there is a whitish and glossily reflective insulating pulp in which are suspended squash-like seeds in rows, a hundred or more per gourd. There is no reason to doubt why seeds cannot reside in their padded and protected house for years on end.

Ornamental gourd vines resemble cucumber vines, and their small yellow flowers are similar. The plants of hard-shell gourds are far more flamboyant in the racing grasp of their vines and the size of their slightly folded sun-cupping leaves, almost a foot across. Each morning white flowers open horizontally a foot above the vines to float there, expectant of pollinating insect, until the morning sun withers away the delicate petals. Successful pollination will be revealed within a few days by a tiny baby gourd no more than an inch long, green and lightly fuzzed with hairs, lying at the end of a long stem on the ground in the protective shade of the broad leaves.

When you grow hard-shell gourds, or more simply large gourds, you enter into a long and complicated process not at first apparent. A field of large maturing gourds suggests the slow and steady growth of capital through interest compounding, rising stock prices, and the appreciating value of real estate. Life is good. Life is abundant. What goes up promises never to come down. In the first days of autumn, as the yellowing leaves submit to the attacks of insects, and as the swelling green shapes peep pregnantly up into the bright sun, a field of still growing vessels promises prosperity and security. This is a crop that does not decay and rot. It keeps for years, even for decades, perhaps even forever, which is to say that it is the perfect crop, or almost perfect crop, suffering only one flaw, which is that you can't eat it. In fact, nothing can eat it. The strong body-odor smell of green hard-shell gourds must convey the same message to chewing creatures with either two or four legs. Keep away. Do not eat. You won't like what you taste, which is what you smell.

In my early years of grand gourd fields supplying the imaginary Gourd Factory, I harvested large gourds before they froze and hung them from the shed rafters. Eventually I discovered that it would be easier to leave them in the field to freeze, a process that speeds up the drying out of the shell, via a stinking phase, and also quickly culls out unripe gourds whose shells collapse after a frost. If left in the field until late October or November the light and now odorless gourds can be packed into plastic mesh feed sacks, with the vines clipped off just above the stem joint, and the sacks stacked against a protective wall back of the house.

The main reason for leaving the sacks outside is a lack of room inside the sheds. There is no room inside the sheds because sacks of gourds from earlier harvests take up all the room. To the outsider none of this may be clear. He may think you have too many gourds. He may wonder why you are explaining that next year you're going to grow a really big crop.

The attraction of the large gourd lies in its being the Primordial Vessel. I have no idea whether the following thoughts have any basis in science or history. I merely take them for gospel. This belief marks me as a gourd person.

In the beginning was the gourd as knapsack, water jug, float, fisherman's bowl, hamper, basket, pouch, drum, soundbox, and as crown of

Pharaoh. The gourd is the great ancestor of the glass bottle, the tin can, the plastic yogurt container. And though I cannot say that I would actually dream of ever storing my water or wine in a gourd, or eating out of a gourd bowl, or keeping my yogurt in a gourd in the refrigerator, or going to town with a gourd strapped to my belt and containing my checkbook and credit cards or with one fitted to my head as a rain hat, I still proclaim the suitability of the gourd for all these uses. Indeed, I will cite one aspect in which it is far superior to all its industrial replacements: it is biodegradable either in the backyard compost pile or in the fireplace, without the need of special processes.

To serve these uses, at least in an aesthetically pleasing manner, the gourd must first be cleaned of its outside skin, a slightly waxy membrane which may serve to add a year or two to the shell's life as a water resistant seedcase, thus increasing opportunities for it to be found, carried off, or swept away. But this waxiness resists most stains, dyes, paints, and oils. Beneath the skin lies a thinner, somewhat more translucent layer which will accept paints and oils. Beneath that is the slightly darker tan of the shell with an extremely fine or tight surface not unlike a fine-grained hardwood. The shell's surface is so unporous that stains do not adhere well, particularly if their pigments are at all granular.

The annals of "The Gourd" are filled with ideas on how to remove the skin easily. I have tried many of these, invented a few myself, but invariably have found myself back at the kitchen sink scrubbing off skin and mold with a wad of coarse steel wool. If the gourds are good and moldy, this can take a couple of minutes. If dry, the gourds not having been soaked or composted in any way, scrubbing can take twenty minutes to a half hour for a large healthy gourd. Gourd skin contains a compound that softens or conditions your own skin so that even in October and November, prime season for chapped hands and painful cracks at the tips of fingers, you need have no fear of spending a couple of hours a day scrubbing gourds.

Washing gourds in the evening is when I do my most serious listening to classical music. I suspect the great composers did not intend their work to help a gourd person pass the time in front of a sink of muddy brown water in which float the strands and flecks of gourd skin, stems, dead leaves, and tendrils.

Yet, there is a result to this sometimes tedious scrubbing, which is why you do it, why you make the mess. The mottled and blotchy skin of a gourd is map enough to lose your thoughts in. What is revealed, skin scrubbed off, is a shadowy version of what was once there. This new, more subtly modulated surface here and there suggests the grain of a redwood burl, or one of Dubuffet's earthy blobs, or healed scars on wood or skin, the surface of bits of bark, or the shifts in tone of a photograph. Surfaces of a remarkable smoothness surround islands of rich coruscation, on a form of slight yet serene asymmetry that only the greatest of potters could duplicate.

In the long scrubbing and palping, I come to know my gourds, assessing the thickness and strength of their shells, and begin to think of whether I will turn them into pots or bird feeders by the way they stand or hang, and also by their size. I often go into an evening of gourd washing with great reluctance, knowing it will end with the drainboard spattered with dirt and bits of skin and puddles of muddy water on the floor, thinking there are far better things to be doing, or that surely this is a task that could be automated in the Gourd Factory—yet, when I finish at eleven, and clean up, and lug a large cardboard carton of freshly scrubbed gourds off to the greenhouse to dry, I am usually re-inspired by the subtle grace of my new little population of homunculi. As I spread them out on the greenhouse floor, I sometimes admit to myself that despite my efforts, there is nothing I can do to improve these remarkable shapes.

The music carries me through this work which some might think demeaning. Yet, as labor, it is little different from that which cuts and cures and polishes the woods of musical instruments, or prepares the gut, the bits of bone and metal, the hides; or not so much different from the labors of those who made the parchment and paper for their scores, the pens and ink. We imagine that the great symphonies and quartets and trios and sonatas were written for and listened to not by the working people but by those who hired them—to scrub gourds, or floors, or laundry, or stables, all day long. But surely the little people would have heard snatches or even whole passages through open doors and windows, through ceilings and floors, and would have known moments of consolation and relief.

I scrub away, sometimes in time with the music, at moments softly so I can hear a favorite melody. Most often I am hardly aware of the brushing sounds of steel wool against the gourd shell, water splashing gently, dripping, the hollow scraping and clonk of gourd against the porcelain sink, or that sound peculiar to a gourd when you place it on the brick floor or let it drop a short distance, a sound both sharp like that made by hard plastic yet also flatly resonant like an underinflated basketball.

With such music, with such shapes in your hands, it is not so terrible a way to spend an evening after all. I scrub away. Now and then I turn on the hot water and rinse off a gourd and run my fingers over it in search of last flecks of skin. Gourd person thoughts wander through my brain. About vessels and time. About how we all live high up in a skyscraper now, even those of us who still grow gourds and who still farm, and how we all inhabit a mental space a hundred stories above the earth. About how we all perch up there with our daily needs supplied by global conduits and pumps, where we can so easily forget about the army of groundlings who supply the materials for our elevated environments. Where we can so easily forget that this vast effort of collective levitation is supported by the climate-altering combustion of nonrenewable fuels and the stripping of forests and oceans everywhere.

How long can the vine of a gourd grow? How high? Does what goes up sooner or later come down? What is the lifetime of our industrial civilization? Will it deflate and crash? Will it outwit the odds that have brought down the great empires, even Pharoah's, even with his crown of gilded gourd? Will it come to its senses and turn back from the shortsightedness that has farmed soil to exhaustion, fouled waterways, created desert and flood? What vast suffering are we storing up for the future in our unthinking ways?

Should I grow more gourds next year?

■

There is nothing grand about the Gourd Factory. No assembly lines, loading docks, soaking vats, pallets, forklifts. The reality is modest, consisting of a few of us sitting around the shed cutting gourds and burning designs on their shells, trimming circles of plastic screen, lengths of fine copper wire, jute twine, and baling wire, rubbing on oil-color stain, rubbing on finishing wax. We do this in the garlic shed or out in the sun in the driveway, the radio playing, and in the greenhouse at night. We do this fitfully, sometimes only a day or two a month, or a couple of hours a night, and sometimes in rushes of several days running. There are son Adam and daughter Kate when they are home in the summer to help out on the farm, there's Kiva Duckworth between semesters at college, there's Lawrence Lucero who has probably made up thousands of gourd strings over the decades; and myself, the scrubber, stainer, and waxer. At best we produce a couple of hundred strings, pots, and bird feeders a year.

They sell fitfully, in funny little bursts that perhaps correspond to the unpredictable migrations of gourd people around the earth. At our retail outlet in Taos, which space we share with friends who are potters and winemakers, Rose Mary is quick to notice them when they come in the door. Unlike most customers, who are drawn to the bottles of wine on the counter or to the garlic braids and bunches hanging from a wall, they will make straight for a gourd pot or bird feeder.

They are always a little startled when they hear her melodious voice call out from behind them: "Oh, you must be gourd people."

|1997| A friend laments that the problem with the endangered Rio Grande silvery minnow is that it's so small. If only it were the size of a whale, then it would get the attention it needs.

Attention, yes. As a society we have become inattentive to Nature, which has become mainly what is on the other side of the window glass, in an outdoors increasingly too hot and too dry. A few may remember that Nature was once the source of our language, our imagery, our dreams and fears. Now we have Windows—95, 98, or 2000. We're inside the box, the house, the office, the car, looking out through the screen, the monitor, through tinted glass darkly. We know more about pixels than silvery minnows or the hundreds of other species that stream surreptitiously through our cities and suburbs and fields and diminished watercourses. Nature no longer feeds our language. We glean our images from baseball, financial reports, movie making, prison life, gangs. We have stopped figuring Nature into the bottom line. We can see the big picture. We can count the pixels. But out of sight, outdoors, the river and its creatures die, because most of us never go there anymore unaccompanied by our machines.

Crisis is what happens when people are inattentive for too long and decide to neglect certain details from their always simplistic calculations. The silvery minnow is one of those details. Will the world end because we drive it into extinction? No. But if we can muster the restraint, the ingenuity, the generosity, even the long-term self-interest to save this and countless other small species from extinction, will the world be a richer and more hopeful place? Surely.

Florida has roused itself to save the Everglades. Even in

water imperialist California, ways have been found to make the Owens River flow again and recharge Mono Lake. Even in Los Angeles, wetlands are being rescued from neglect and being saved from development.

Power corrupts. Power renders people inattentive, stupid. Each day, temperatures rising, rainfall in decline, Nature is telling us to be more attentive, to be more generous, to relinquish some of our dangerous power. We water our lawns and our fields with subsidized water—subsidized not just by taxpayers but also because environmental costs were not factored in when those grand systems were constructed. At the time nobody thought that the silvery minnow or the willow flycatcher really mattered. The world was for people, cars, and cows. Even the majestic cottonwood groves, which are New Mexico's easily visible whale equivalents, were slated for clearcutting from San Juan Pueblo to Soccoro twenty years ago under the notorious Phreatophyte Eradication Program.

Let us hope we've grown a little wiser since then. Silvery minnow, that should be an easy one. Under traditional Spanish water law, which once reigned all over the state, when the water was low, all shared. There was no winner takes all.

We humans are creatures with the ability to destroy the world—and ourselves. But we are also unique in our powers of imagination and empathy. If we choose to, we can enter into the human-created plight of the silvery minnow. As my gardening neighbors like to say, you have to plant enough seed not just for yourself but also for *los animalitos*, the little creatures.

The little creatures, *los animalitos*, are the ones that really count, because they are the ones by which we can measure our capacity as human beings—for attentiveness, for empathy, for vision, and for hope.

|2000| More ravens. Fewer vultures. Hardly any toads at all. Coyotes yodeling at dusk at the bottom of the drive as never before. A first bear sighted climbing the hill.

As someone who spends a fair amount of each day outdoors minding gardens and fields, these are some of the recent changes I have noted. The dogs have no doubt seen much more. They sit sphinx-like for hours on end in our driveway turnaround and stare up at the steep bluff above the garlic shed, noses pointed up at a forty-five-degree angle, as if they're watching TV. What they await is the fleeting movement between juniper trees or the sound of pebble or rock dislodged by a jackrabbit or a coyote, signal for them to bound up the steps and across the acequia and begin scrambling up the gravelly slope.

They are our scouts out into the wild world. Both have returned from the hillside or emerged from the brush along the river reeking of skunk or with gashes in their flanks. Most recently our German Shepherd 'Budo returned with a three-inch wound in his side. In retrospect, the likely culprit was a bear, come down into the valley for a pre-hibernation feast of apples, and very possibly the same bear that Rose Mary discovered the dogs pursuing up the bluff a few weeks later, in time to call them back and prevent further injury. The bear, she reported, was walking on its hind legs up the slope. We later learned that our bear tapped on the window of a friend's house one night and was later blamed for pulling sheets and other laundry off their clothesline and that of other friends further down the river. The bear with a laundry fetish.

The Embudo Valley is an important migratory corridor for other creatures, especially birds. You can tell the time, as it were, by who's moving through. Bluebirds and robins heading for higher elevations in the spring—or retreating back down in bad weather. Warblers of various kinds pausing in late summer and early fall to scour the sunflower stalks for tiny insects. Sandhill cranes circling overhead through swirling clouds of autumn storms, heading south for the winter. Turkey vultures carried north on spring storms and reassembling on cottonwood snags where they have roosted for generations, perhaps for eons. They are eventually joined by summer-only residents: killdeer, flycatchers, nighthawks, swifts and swallows, whose arrival is timed to the breeding cycles of insects in the warming days and nights.

Coyotes are here all year round and have become more vocal and bolder, even casual. It used to be that we could count on an occasional sighting during one of our autumn wood runs. Now I see them every week or so, often in broad daylight, in relatively populated areas. Ravens, once rare, will now and then assemble into flocks of a hundred or more on a neighbor's manicured lawn, in a sort of "parlement of fowles," object of medieval fascination. They claim a niche similar to the more domestic magpies, which hold treetop parliaments in late summer. Along with scrub jays, they are thieves of dog and cat food and, worse, raiders of songbird nests. Opportunistic species, weed species, omnivors—rather like humans themselves.

Less aggressive, shyer residents are juncos, chickadees, towhees, and various kinds of sparrows. Nuthatches reveal themselves by wheezy little musings as up side down they explore tree trunks and eaves. Down at the river mallards regularly appear, the occasional blue heron and kingfisher, and sparrow hawks and larger hawks I am so excited to see that I make poor note of their markings; and once or twice only, a bald eagle. Water ouzels (or the American dipper bird) are present whenever there is a good enough flow for their underwater foragings, but their manner of perching on a rock and dipping up and down while uttering a sharp call, comes as a taunt to 'Budo, who crashes into the icy water in futile pursuit.

In the days when we kept chickens, ducks, geese, guinea fowl, rabbits, and goats, we had another relation to the wildlife, as defenders of our herds and flocks. I once helped a neighbor transport a bobcat trapped in their henhouse up the hill where from the back of my pickup we released it, an arrow shooting out of the cage. After forays by weasels and skunks and neighboring dogs, we installed lights for the vulnerable dark hours. These kept most predators at bay—except a large demented or sick owl which killed a goose in the early hours of the morning and except the increasingly bold coyotes who finished off the entire flock of geese during evenings when I had returned exhausted from town business day after day. A pair of very charming and witty packrats—they look like huge mice with lovely ears and large liquid eyes—once systematically stripped ristras hanging from the shed rafters of their chile, using the bright red pods to line a couple of spare tires on the floor, until I reluctantly caught them and exiled them to separate ends of the valley.

One creature once common is now missing: the toad. It used to be that whenever we left an outside light on in the summer, a toad or two would sit underneath it and pick off the swarming insect life. I had to be on the lookout for them when tilling under cover crops with the tractor, often stopping to scoop one up and carry it to the edge of the field. But no more. Toads are as rare as coyotes once were.

Opportunistic species may be taking advantage of our abandonments. In these parts people live and work outdoors much less than they used to. Only one or two families keep small herds of cattle, down from a half dozen or more a generation ago. The once familiar and troubling sounds of a Saturday morning *matanza,* the prolonged squealing of a pig ending in a gunshot, are no longer heard in the neighborhood. A few neighbors still keep sheep, chickens, geese, but the valley no longer echoes with their sounds. Only horses, conducting lonely vigils in their pastures, have retained their former numbers.

But perhaps they too, like the dogs, are observing all the minute events that the rest of us, in our haste, mostly no longer bother to notice. Perhaps this is why in the summer, when the weather warms, I always take the time to walk down to the river and sit for awhile in the shallow water, ostensibly to cool down, but also to learn how to be patient again, to become curious and observant, like the fingerling trout that sometimes brush against and pick at my feet. With luck, slowed down, I will again imagine the universe of the ant exploring the gravel or the tiny white spider that spins an invisible catwalk of webbing between blades of grass.

And now and then, being still and observant, dogs dozing in the shade of the willows, I will be privy to an event I may never see again, as when a tiny larva twirled up from the bottom of my pool, broke the surface and sloughed off its skin to reveal the graceful translucent wings of a mayfly. All in a flash, right before my eyes, the creature took flight.

IV THE INFRASTRUCTURE OF PLACE

|2001| Once upon a time the Santa Fe Farmers' Market was what I call a "Zucchini Market."

A Zucchini Market is what takes place after your refrigerator is full of zucchini, and after your friends and neighbors begin refusing generous gifts of zucchini, and after the chickens begin pecking at other things. This is when the collective intelligence declares that it's time to start opening up the Farmers' Market.

Recent arrivals to Santa Fe are astounded when I tell them that back in the 1970s the Farmers' Market didn't open until the last week in July, which is when zucchini, corn, and beans begin producing in abundance.

Mind you, this was before salad was introduced into Northern New Mexico. The question of how to pronounce *arugula* was still fifteen years off. Greenhouses, cold frames, and row covers were still the subject of theory and rumor. Farm equipment dealers had not yet begun to import compact diesel tractors designed with the small farmer in mind. It would be another twenty years before eggs, meat, cheese, and farm-based processed foods and crafts were allowed into the market.

In the intervening decades, a technological revolution in small-scale agriculture has rippled through northern New Mexico, enabling the Farmers' Market to open up a week earlier every two years or so, gradually expanding to a seven-month-plus season that now runs from late April until mid-November. Such changes may eventually enable it to operate year-round, particularly when its fifth and finally permanent site is constructed in the Railyard—with good paving, some shelter, and electrical outlets for heaters and lights.

The peak of the season remains September. This is when the first big brown burlap sacks of chile are brought to the market and when the chile roasters—a nifty folk invention—are fired up, sending plumes of fragrant smoke wafting through the market. The senses awaken. The pace quickens. The first boxes and bushel baskets of apples also appear and the first jugs of freshly pressed apple cider. At the beginning of the month farmers will begin creating piles of the first winter squash, acorn, eventually to be followed by butternut and buttercup and kabocha squash and a half dozen varieties of pumpkin.

September is the month of maximum variety. Though apricots and cherries and asparagus are now memories, there is still sweet corn and green beans and summer squash and cucumbers and tomatoes and melons and onions and garlic and leeks, all in their prime, plus flowers still in abundance; and often the best greens can be grown in the cooling nights of September, when the sated bugs have retired to lay their eggs for overwintering—at least the ones that have survived burgeoning populations of birds.

The summer of 2001 marked the first time in twenty years that I have not been at the Farmers' Market every Saturday, either as a farmer or as a Farmers' Market functionary. No more getting up at 4 AM, climbing in the pickup at 5, arriving in Santa Fe at 6, trying to get set up by 7. But Rose Mary and I had it easy compared to Jake and Leona West in Fort Sumner, who have to get up at 2 AM in order to bring their melons to the market in time.

There is much I miss. Experiencing from beginning to end the miracle of this supermarket-for-a-day assembling itself in the pre-dawn dark and swelling to the size of a small garrulous town and then vanishing again by 1 in the afternoon. Piloting an old pickup laden with the best produce in the world down through the Española Valley, in the light of a harvest moon beginning to slip behind the Jemez Mountains— though not the return drive, battling late morning traffic, fatigue, thirst, and the leaden hangover of the workaholic.

A farmers' market is an extended family. In the course of the long days selling at the market year after year and decade after decade, setting up and tearing down, you get to know your customers as they shop and your fellow farmers as they work, in complex and unexpected ways.

In recent years a new crop of farmer babies has been bouncing around in the back packs of their parents, coming into consciousness among the eyes and hands and words of the market family, amid crates and tables and umbrellas and pickups of the thriving scene. People bring kids to the Farmers' Market because it's real, stimulating, fun, and safe.

And the absent and the departed hover over it all: founders and first managers Cornelia Hull, Palemón Martínez, Julia Carlsen, and Lupe Romero; farmer Truman Brigham, who came to the Española Valley as a young man and sold at the market from its establishment in 1970 until the fall of 1997, holding out until a Sunday after the market to leave us all. Mrs. Vigil, expert grower of gladioli, who packed her aging white Chevy Carryall with blooms well into her eighties. Amadeo Trujillo of Nambé Pueblo, whose daughter Gloria now carries on the tradition. Market treasurer and retired Los Alamos physicist and fellow University of Chicago graduate David Hall, whose very last errand was at the service of the Farmers' Market. Arnie Souder, tough but beloved volunteer market manager, until Pam Roy took over as the market's first full-time staffer and continued on as director of Friends of the Farmers' Market and indefatigable community builder.

By September, farmers and customers both will know whether this is a good or bad water year, good or bad fruit year, or one of those seasons when new varieties of insects decide to feast on the fat of the land or when wilt will decimate tomato and chile crops. The first cold and rainy market days can have one of two effects: customers either stay at home, not up to facing the elements, or else they turn out in droves, to stock up against the approaching winter. For Rose Mary and me, October was always our best Farmers' Market month. Our record day was a sopping wet October morning when umbrella-jousting customers bought up everything in sight. As one of them said, "I was lying in bed all snug and warm and thinking of you standing in the rain with all that great produce, so I just had to get up and come on down."

For the most part, the days of the bloated five-pound zucchini are long gone, and small, tender, flavorful summer squash are now the rule. And of course, even squash blossoms have entered the menu.

In the good old days of the Zucchini Market, who would have guessed?

|2001| Woe to he who would move to the country seeking peace and quiet.

True, between phone calls, meetings, and callers-in, there may be a few bucolic moments, when the air is still and balmy and the garden in flower and the trees are heavy with fruit, and instead of the sound of traffic the rush of water fills the air, from the acequia, or the stream, or the river. True, these are moments to live for, and to come home for.

But the larger reality is that the small places of the world are run on the backs of the unpaid, the underpaid, and the volunteer. I know: I have been there. In my village there is no one who serves the needs of the village who is overpaid by any state or national standard. Among Post Office, elementary school, clinic, and two of the four churches there are some thirty full-time jobs with full benefits, serving the 2400 people who live in the Embudo Valley and its outlying hamlets. Add to this the part-time "salaries" received by nine or ten acequia mayordomos and the public library director and there you have the total public sector paid employment of the valley.

This is something, but it is not everything. The rest of the village has to be run by volunteers. There is the volunteer fire department. The acequia commissions. The boards of the mutual domestic water associations. The library board. The Dixon Studio Tour board. The volunteer groups that support the schools, the churches, and the clinic. Plus ad hoc groups that assemble to deal with threats of mining in the hills or expansion of the ski valley or to advise the county on land use and water planning and trash collection and recycling and the perpetual threat of re-routing or widening this or that highway or paving or not paving this or that back road. Logging on nearby public lands. Grazing. Recreation. Water rights adjudication. Fire prevention. Flood prevention. Sooner or later most northern New Mexico villages have to negotiate with the federal Bureau of Land Management, the Corps of Engineers, the Forest Service, the Soil Conservation Service, and the New Mexico State Engineer Office, Fish and Wildlife Service, and the Highway Department, plus various county departments. Almost exclusively, it is volunteers who do this work, through groups that form and reform, dissolve and come back to life, depending on the urgency of the threat.

I know. At one time or another over the past thirty years I have belonged to most of them. Even had a hand in founding a few. There was the short-lived film society, in the pre-video days, which showed three classics in the fire house. There was the Dixon Community Forum which, under Janet Greenwald's scolding, coalesced into the first organized opposition to the Waste Isolation Pilot Plant near Carlsbad, the nuclear waste dump carved out of subterranean salt beds.

Under its umbrella I published *El Mes en Dixon*, a monthly calendar of Embudo Valley events, featuring images created by local artists and schoolchildren and, drawn from historical sources, old maps and photographs of the valley and relics such as a timetable from the Denver & Rio Grande Western Chile Line narrow gauge trains, which stopped at the present Embudo Station twice daily up until 1940.

My intentions were mildly boosterish, to counter the poor self-image this small place, like many, often suffers from. The agenda of any city daily newspaper is to celebrate and promote and memorialize the *polis* through countless images and the printed word. A village often lacks the means: stories are forgotten, records go up in flames (as when the Catholic Church burned in the 1920s), private photographs and documents are dispersed to the four winds, if not bagged up and hauled to the dump. Until the Embudo Valley Library was founded in late 1980s, the area was effectively without its own archive.

Schoolchildren and local artists were surprisingly forthcoming with images for the broadsheet. One of the best and craziest was a scratchboard drawing by Ken MacDonald for the July 1982 issue, entitled "30 Seconds Over Dixon," reflecting the paranoia and odd goings-on of the contentious period of BLM land claim disputes and mysterious cattle mutilations. The night scene shows three flying saucers shooting presumably mutilating rays down on cattle and a BLM transport flying upside down ("out of control"?) above a fleet of drug-delivering helicopters and amid mysterious giant arrows shooting through the black sky.

After a few years of living in a small place, you become connected to virtually everyone else in the village, if even tenuously, at several removes. When the bell tolls in the city, the city dweller will breeze through the obituaries to see if it's anyone he knows; but in the village, when the bell tolls, you either know exactly who it is or else you find out by asking your neighbor or the shopkeeper. In time, after a decade of two, a necropolis of all those who have died in the village can take up residence in your imagination, along with a vivid catalogue of how: by car wreck, drowning, shooting, slow wasting away and out in a flash in the garden, on the dance floor, in sleep.

The seeds of disputes over history and real estate in Northern Ireland, Kosovo, Bosnia, Palestine, and innumerable other places—these germs, these viruses lie dormant in the unresolved quarrels and feuds of any village, hidden within differences in age, ethnicity, language, sexual orientation. Villages, like cities, can teach either tolerance or intolerance. But a village can also offer a useful lesson: that the man you may quarrel with today may have to help put out the fire or repair the acequia next to you tomorrow. And he will probably be among those you shake hands with at a funeral. At the very least, you will run into him again and again at the post office or the village store. The village says: Deal with it.

Since there are no concentrations of wealth in one person or family in the village, it means that everyone sooner or later can have a place in the rotations of power. It takes some work not to be elected to your acequia commission. Sooner or later the young hotheads come to power—and find themselves becoming cautious, smooth-talking functionaries. The great bureaucracies of our times—those of the federal government—are remote and inscrutable to most people, at least a few of whom are willing to project their frustrations on to their elected neighbors, blaming them for the ills and injustices of their lives. Any volunteer village official is bound to wonder if his most useful function may be therapeutic. The thing to do is listen. And listen.

Above all, the village wants you to participate. Not too much, not with ambition, not to become prominent, not as a know-it-all who tries to tell other people what to do. In return, the village will not give much in the way of thanks, knowing perhaps how easy we all have it now, in the early years of the twenty-first century with all our telephones and cars and computers and paved roads and electricity and fancy medical techniques. All so much more than they had in the old days, when New Mexico was still *new* to the first European settlers. And hard. And dangerous. And unforgiving.

In the old days, the village knew that it takes a village to run a village. It still hasn't forgotten.

You never know, it says. Just in case. These may be good times, it says, but just when have they ever lasted forever?

| 1995 | The gesture is this: you shake your head and stare into space—at the seemingly foolish or self-destructive behavior of some neighbors or one of the village clans or even members of some local organization who have come to blows, verbal, physical, legal.

Do all villages feud?

It would seem so. You hear stories. Almost incomprehensible versions of them appear in local papers—incomprehensible because of what cannot be written or spoken publicly but which everyone in the village or small town knows. You pick up the phone and call a friend in another village fifty miles away whose feuding has reached the local papers and you ask, "So what's all that about?" The recall of a school board member, the resignation of a commissioner, shots fired through a window, outcries over a public works project. In a few words your friend explains it all. The details always seem as universal as human nature itself. Afterward, putting the phone down, you think, well, maybe we're not so bad after all.

Of course these things go on at the national level, but we won't learn all the grubby details for a generation or more, when the personal papers are unsealed and the biographies written and published. In a small place, there is no waiting. You hear about it the same day or next week or in a month at the latest, from the gossip network of phone calls and encounters at the post office, the store, the library, and during the milling around before and after meetings in the school gym and during the daily senior citizens' lunch sessions.

The secret life of the village is a rich fabric woven out of conversations taking place somewhere all day long and every day, conversations fretted over and dreamed about and imagined, with friends and enemies and neighbors and co-workers. In this collective verbal labor, we all bear names and descriptions we will never hear, nicknames that everyone in town knows except the bearer. There are currents of private scandal made up of the gleanings of things let slip or revealed in unguarded moments of pain or grief or passion or desperation or drunkenness, which we may naively believe that no one else but ourselves is privy to—even after we have confided to others. Here in this vast unwritten book are recorded all the ancient slights and omissions, cheatings, deceptions, swindles, and our seven deadly sins, often worn and twisted into unrecognizable shapes, as they are passed from hand to hand, perhaps even tinted with details from soap operas from those TVs which remain on all day long and through half the night.

The book is endless. Were all the inhabitants of a village to pour out their thoughts and memories, emptying the vast silos of the collective gossip mill, the tale would be without end, a complaint with intricately spiraling justifications and no solace, yet studded with neat examples of cause and effect of the sort considered to be generally absent from the muddle of human affairs. It is this grand collective novel that all feuders and litigants tap into—much as in the heat of battle a quarreling couple revivifies quibbles thought long ago forgotten and summons up grievances that have been quietly nursed against the eventuality.

The secret agenda of all feuding may be that no quarrel can ever be settled. The tale, the village novel, must never end. We feud, therefore we live—even as we lie awake at three and four in the morning seeking justice or revenge or even forgetfulness. This collective labor demands a continual supply of new material in order to refresh the old, in order to extend the circle wider and wider in time and space, towards a universality that all art aspires to. It is through our gossip, our telling of tales, through our collective village novel that we will finally establish that we live at the center of the universe—however insignificant this small place may seem to the great wide world.

A pleasure travelers can experience from a small place is to have all its secrets confided to them by a friendly local informant. There is a nice exchange here: the villager puts his place on the mental map of the urban visitor, winning a subtle victory of self-esteem in this betrayal of all his neighbors. This sidelong maneuver allows him to privately violate the taboo against publishing the village novel and settle scores without fear of reprisal. Conveniently, all evidence of hypocrisy is packed up and departs with the traveler.

Writers who grow up hearing episodes and chapters of the village novel at the knees of parents and grandparents and aunts and uncles set out into the literary world with something far better than a formal education—but this is also the source of the grief they can suffer when they offer up the contents of the village novel as a real book, a novel. They will then be charged with betraying confidences and appropriating something that belongs to no one person, or for quite simply getting it all wrong. This is the theft Faulkner spoke of when he said all writers are "thieves and liars." As a precaution, Joyce advised "exile and cunning." A *fatwa* awaits all who dare retail the village secrets to the outside world.

The unwritten novel of a small place can seem at times to be a miasma of ill-will, grudge, narrow-mindedness, low-level blackmail, a dark parody of the life of reason and tolerance we all like to believe we lead. What is this obsessive vigilance? Who are these verbal vigilantes? What is this passion for pettiness really about? And what is this strange power of the whisper, the thing said behind your back, the constant zooming in on the feet of clay, the exasperating power of gossip to ostracize and even banish, what is the nature of the power the village summons up to stone its own prophets?

In totalitarian states fiction is feared for its power to undermine ideological certainties with ridicule and to overwhelm them with encyclopedias of all-too-human exceptions in the form of renegades, oddballs, misfits, whose humanity can sabotage the most perfect ideas. The gossip mill is the indigenous power structure of the disempowered, the disenfranchised, the weak and marginalized, employing the acid of fiction and parody to eat away the bright plating of official pretense wherever it appears: folk art with a vengeance. Kant's dictum can serve as a guiding principle: "From the crooked timber of mankind, nothing straight has ever been cut."

The gossipers' skills are exercised broadly and indiscriminately against pretension in all its forms, and against falseness and deception, even while employing falseness and hypocrisy as means. The gossiper, like the secret policeman, sees everyone's life as an open book. Because the accused is always absent, gossip lacks fairness or justice or even reason, except where they serve the needs of the gossiper. Gossip is rarely benevolent. It is most often malicious, which is to say coercive.

There is much cruelty in all wars for the soul of a place. Don Quixote did battle with villagers, who mocked his idealism with their home truths. And yet his grand, cracked story has turned out to be victorious over theirs. We go to the book, or to the place, in search of the soul of this crazed man, knowing how much we share in his divine silliness. We don't go to seek out the earthy wisdom of those who dismissed him as nothing more than a madman—because we know that they are the baggage that so firmly tethers us to earth. We read his life on his side, not on theirs.

Sometimes I think that the power of this thing, the collective novel of the village in which I play the part of a character I can never know and a contributor whose words I immediately lose control of, explains everything that seems to go wrong in a small place: the self-inflicted wounds, the scapegoating and witch-hunting, the stifling of initiative, the inability to cooperate in a positive way.

Yet the ability to quarrel and feud is granted only to those who have made a prior agreement about what is important. The village itself is this area of common interest and the subject of contention. Gossiping and feuding are twin sisters. Their fastidious attention to detail, which is the novelist's skill, organizes the knowledge of a place and its people like nothing else. Every firmly rooted person possesses this knowledge. In traditional societies, it includes the names and uses of every kind of vegetation and the lore of wildlife within a topography indistinguishable from history and legend and cosmology. It is easy to forget how new is our ability to look at a landscape for pure aesthetic pleasure, and to plant gardens and parks as things to look at, unencumbered with encrustations of local lore, mythology, and history.

Modern life requires most of us to live in two or three places at once: where we were born and raised, where we have settled, and some place in mainstream commercial America or in any one of the nearly identical parallel flows it seems to be breaking into, some real, some virtual. Even inhabitants of still somewhat traditional villages are mobile and connected now. They share in the roving habits of the elite who have found out how to excuse themselves from all the world's feuds. The mobile drive by them, they fly over them, sail around them, surf away from them, lock gates against them, and generally don't stick around long enough in one place to become rooted. The mobile do not know any one place well enough to gossip or feud, which gives them reason to hold in contempt those who still engage in these old-fashioned practices. Our modern ways are dismissive of the human soul of place. The bulldozers come next. Then the theme parks, which attempt to replace place with something that can be more easily managed and profited from.

The collective village novel may be about control and by extension about the environment itself. It studies how the social machinery of the village ought to work, how it actually works, where it threatens to break down, and how the village interacts with the natural world in which it is embedded, with animals and plants, the river, the acequias and arroyos, the forests on the high ground above it, and its gods. The village knows what the city can forget, that its life is deeply affected by how it cares for its place. It knows, if confusedly at times, that if it abuses its water, forests, croplands, then it endangers its own health and survival. Gossip and feuding are signals that the village is still alert and vigilant and that it will accept change, or certain changes, only very slowly.

Perhaps there is a deep deceptiveness here. The complex truth of a place, a collective creation stretched out over generations which is its greatest treasure, must be protected at all costs from the outsider, from the colonist, from the proselytizer, the exploiter, the anthropologist, the writer. In this, even the unreliability of gossip may serve. The collective village novel is fiction in order to conceal the essential core of truth about a place, the beating heart, the soul, the hidden spring of passion. Gossip may be the fabric in which the village hides its greatest secret, which is known only to the weavers of the tapestry, as seen only in the inverse shadows behind, the side never shown to the outside world.

And could the feuding be also intended to lull the outsider into thinking that the place and its squabbling inhabitants are weak and divided? No doubt feuds have destroyed villages and towns and whole societies everywhere in the world and continue to do so. Yet they can also be seen as sport, as games, as practice, perhaps for that occasion when the village must unite and focus itself against the powerful outsider. A village, after all, knows more about itself than busloads of outside experts. When unleashed, a village's scorn and mockery can break the composure of even the most seasoned bureaucrats. I have seen the careers of Forest Service and highway department and mining company bureaucrats falter and perhaps even crash at public meetings in the school gym.

The village is practiced in the tough battle for survival, for which outsiders with their often naïve plans and simplistic ideas can find themselves no match. A small place must wage constant battle against the great cities of the world, which are always sending emissaries to try to take its land for roads, its water for downstream suburbs and golf courses, its forests for the corporations, and its children as helots for its wars abroad. The village's long and painful experience teaches it to beware of the warm-sounding buzzwords of the era: cooperation, tolerance, reason. In its sharp and bristling way it may be saying that place and home are not negotiable.

Yet, against all expectation, a village is not a hive of misanthropic recluses. It gathers itself together again and again, in weddings and funerals, in sports events at the school, in the latest version of the village fair, in parties and dances, and at meetings and hearings.

This is when it shows its public face, not always united, rarely speaking with one voice, but saying nonetheless, to use the words of Robert Frost: "To socialize is to forgive."

|1995| "What we do best here is funerals," a friend once confided wryly to me on the portal of the Catholic church. We were looking down on the scene of a casket being wheeled into a metallic gray hearse.

I suppressed a smile. I knew what he meant. In a small place where things so often fail, where neighbors often have trouble working together and where dreams so often evaporate, funerals succeed in what they are supposed to do. They get something done. The dead are sent off and are buried. And that is that.

When you live in a village, you see the same people nearly every day. You see them first as babies, then as children, then as youths, then as adults and parents themselves. They move away. They move back and re-introduce themselves. "Remember me? I'm so-and-so's son." You watch the young fill out into middle age. You watch their middle-aged parents twist into old age, you watch the grandparents wither and die. You see others die, too, at any age. And in the reflection of other lives and deaths, you watch yourself moving through the ages of mankind towards your own death.

When you live in one place long enough, pockets of darkness lengthen into shadows and cast a pall over everything, over the houses and fields and orchards lining the road, like a passing cloud or an eclipse. This shadow is a necropolis. It is inhabited by all the people of your place who have died in your time.

I'm not a careful custodian of my necropolis. I don't find death a subject of fascination or even entertainment, as some do. I avoid all funerals I can fabricate an excuse not to attend.

I'm no fan of the obituary page. The names of the dead do not populate my journal, with the exception of those few I have been close to or have worked with. There was the goat-raising woman who became an early friend in the village. The mechanic who kept all our cars going for many years. An old mayordomo who came home after a day working on the acequia and lay down on his couch and died. My wife's too young best friend whose heart gave out while dancing on a New Year's Eve.

But given a day or two and perhaps a visit to the four village cemeteries, I could repopulate my necropolis with those who have died in car wrecks, drownings, shooting incidents, and those who were murder victims and suicides, those who died young, or relatively young, from cancer, stroke, heart attack, cirrhosis of the liver, aneurysm, and all those who died of old age. Three or four a year over twenty-five years. Perhaps a hundred in all. Perhaps more.

There are nameless others from the past who have had a strange bearing on our lives here. There was the boy killed by a falling cottonwood down by the river. The event placed a curse on the land for the family, who eventually sold it to my wife and me.

Another woman tried to erase the memory of a village feud that ended in murder and prison terms for a father and uncles when she sold us a field across the river, cutting the connection between the village and her adopted home in southern Colorado. The last time she looked at the land before signing the papers, she said, "The devil lives in this valley." On that sloping, rocky field we now grow winter squash and gourds. Often, while gleaning the last gourds in the lowering light of October, bending over, I catch sight of the tall poplar trees of the place across the highway, uphill from the field. The trees are perfectly familiar and ordinary, yet when I am stooped over, with my back to them, and glimpse them out of the corner of my eye, there is something ominous about them. Out of the corner of the eye, this is how it will finally happen. How death will approach. From behind, as a shadow.

The village teaches you the hard lesson that you have to die, and the village funeral is where you know you cannot escape your fate. It is where you will hear the official truths called out from the pulpit or the graveside. You will learn the more instructive details on how to die, and how not, in murmured remarks before or after. The very young may not trouble to work through the terrible logic of the situation, in which certain proof is offered that sooner or later everyone's turn will come—unless the body in the open casket is a young victim of a moment of carelessness or miscalculation.

The village buries its own dead. Its necropolises, as physical places, are not far from where the living carry on their daily business. My village favors barren slopes up arroyos, in landscapes of stunted piñon and juniper trees and cactus and dry grass and rocks and gravel and sand, places that mock the polished shoes and nylon stockings and shiny new cars of relations come back from distant cities. Faces may be twisted in grief—or they may only be squinting in the bright sun, or fretting about stepping on cactus, or getting scratches on new paint, or at the discomfort of unaccustomed clothes, or calculating how long it will take to get back to the parish hall and spread the food out on the table, or how long before one can step away for a smoke, a drink, or to take a leak, or to pull off the dark hood of grief and joke and laugh again.

Perhaps one of the reasons people leave villages all over the world is that they want to live in places where the lesson is not so relentlessly taught. Suburbs are places without graveyards, without necropolises. They zone out the dead. Like garbage and sewage, the dead are ferried away to special ghettos elsewhere—or anywhere. The modern liberal solution of scattering ashes to the wind seems to solve the problem nicely. By making the dead disappear in a puff of gray ash, we can conquer death itself. Or is it rather just another technological solution that solves nothing, heaping instead the whole matter on to the heads of each of us as isolated individuals? Through our evasions, we may end up dying far more alone than ever. For lack of a familiar necropolis, that village or city where we will take up our final residence, we fall into the void, our ashes dropping from an airplane into a dark and unfamiliar sea.

The reasoning that excluded me as a child from family funerals saw them as threatening to the illusions that the young were thought to need—the adults perhaps not understanding that their children, who are their hopes, should be there to help nurse them and be nursed by them though these dark passages.

When open and generous and inclusive, Catholics are better at funerals than many: something for eyes, for the nose, for ears, and for the tongue, to remind the living that they still live. An evening Rosary in my village can be a bright occasion, with traditional New Mexico songs sung and strummed from the balcony, and where the dressed-up young make eyes at each other in defiance of the occasion, as they must, because they are young and alive and filled with confidence that this cannot be their true business, at least not yet. They are there, restless, hungry, sleepy, thirsty, cranky, curious, prankish, as only the young can be. As they must be.

The village knows that the dead never entirely die. Indeed, they must not be allowed to. They must remain present, guiding custom and tradition—though often mis-leading, just like the living, just as they did in their lives. Because memory is so intimately connected to place, a village can be seen a system for maintaining collective memory within a band of time three or four generations long, between the living present and that time in the past when memory has nothing left to feed on except documentary record. The village necropolis, a repository of names and dates and genealogy and therefore stories, forms an elaborate mnemonic device. To visit an actual graveyard is to be besieged by the clamor of stories to be remembered and retold.

The oldest people in my village are in their nineties, born at the turn of the twentieth century when New Mexico was still a Territory. They are the last generation to speak little or no English. Some of them perhaps still hold memories passed on to them by their parents and grandparents of the coming of the narrow gauge railroad a few miles down the river in the 1880s and of the hard times during the logging of the forests above for railroad ties when logs and ties were floated down the river in flood. They might still recall the havoc this must have wrought on the acequias. Perhaps one or two among these ninety-year-olds has a flickering memory, second or third hand, of the massacre of 1847, the Battle of Embudo Pass, when the territory was seized from Mexico. Perhaps one of them remembers descriptions of Señor Dixon, the Confederate veteran turned schoolteacher and postmaster, who dropped his harsh two-syllable name over the mellifluous Castillian *El Puerto del Embudo de Nuestro Señor San Antonio*. Perhaps some of the old ones once knew Tewa or Tiwa or Apache or even Comanche, and perhaps this is what I hear in the soft nasally accents of some of the old voices. Perhaps they climbed the bluffs above the village to barter with Native Americans camped there, into times within living memory of some of our seventy-year-olds.

Yet the necropolis cannot rule absolutely. Even while we feed from the carcasses of the dead and walk upon the composted detritus of the lives of countless generations of other creatures, we eagerly excuse ourselves from the dark side of the cyclic business. To live without memory is to deny one's mortality; yet life is the continuous, remarkable denial of death. And to live without memory is to embrace the belief that if you can only keep up you will live forever—if only you can keep moving, driving, flying, walking, keep doing anything. We move, therefore we live.

We deny, therefore we live. Even as we know that just out of sight, somewhere behind us, the necropolis awaits our enrollment.

And in this one last collective action, we know the village will be successful. We will be sent off, buried, leaving all the dreams and failures and messiness to the living, and that will be that.

|1991| Meetings.

Sensations of dryness, stuffiness, clamminess surge up, images of windows sealed closed and doors with automatic closers, drapery and blinds, linoleum and blotchy carpet, men in sports coats and ties, women in skirts and pantyhose and white blouses, and the sound of long wrangling conversations marked by scornful laughter and voices rising in disagreement; and the strange presence of those who sit mute through it all. All the while time blinks away later into the morning or afternoon or evening, time lost, time wasted, time thrown away into the bland stew of public life, time stolen from solitude or from the company of family and friends, from food, from drink, from touch, from gazing into the fireplace, from a garden, from a river.

To go to a meeting is to sweep away a list of things you would rather be doing in the company of those you would rather be doing them with. Why most people don't go to most meetings.

Meetings. You don't go because you believe nothing good can come of them. You believe the world is cast in its present form behind closed doors by powers great and high, not by those lesser bodies whose gatherings you can attend and make a noise at. You don't go because you are shy and find it difficult to speak in public, when there are always so many articulate people who can speak for hours without notes. Because you would rather live in world shaped by your own making and by your own wishful thinking than by the grimy negotiations of disreputable politicians at inconvenient times. You don't go because you know that whatever they do it won't have much effect on your life. You don't go. Simply, you don't go.

The individual alone is without power. Meetings are about power. You meet with others in meetings and out of meetings to acquire power, to magnify it, to barter it, to transform it, to project it, to accumulate it. You attend meetings to defend yourself from the effects of power being exercised by others, to frustrate their designs, their plans, to effect the diffusion and transfer of power.

Meetings are about order. Unbridled power ends in anarchy, in violence, death, disintegration. Wherever you see death and destruction ruling the day and night, you know that this is the final effect of unbridled power. Meetings are where power and order negotiate with each other, to strike the bargain of continuity, which often flies under the banner of the status quo, inertia, and the undramatic disintegration of neglect and loss of imagination, leading to rigidity, sclerosis, ossification. Meetings are about whether to change or whether not to change. In meetings things are changed that ought not to be changed, and not changed that cry out for reform. All the world's mistakes have been made in meetings. The battlefields came later.

Power? Order? Change? In a world of mind, of spirit, in a world not material, none of this matters. If you have the willpower and the imaginative power that makes you at home in these other worlds, you will be envied for your otherworldliness. You will have found an answer.

But out of consistency, the answer will call for you to give up the trappings of material privilege, which are the filterings down of the exercise of power ultimately on your behalf, in the form of a roof over your head, food on the table, a car to drive, a television to watch, and nights to sleep and dream undisturbed by the racket of artillery shells and bombs and screams in the darkness outside.

When you renounce these things, then at last you will have no need to go to meetings.

|1993| My own notebooks: this is where I go first.

They're not on a bookshelf. They lean up against the wall next to my armchair, within easy reach. Planting records, harvest records, weather observations, equipment maintenance logs. Plus, perhaps the most important, a loose leaf notebook entitled "Field Notes," a collection of random observations and exhortations about planting and harvesting practices and problems, many of the please-don't-forget-to-do-that-one-more-time variety. A lot of them have to do with running the tractor, the rototiller, the cultivator, and any one of the two planters and two transplanters we use on the farm. Some of the basic records I have maintained over twenty years, but it was only about ten years ago that I discovered the usefulness of narrative records: they read better than mere numbers. I go back to them usually when I'm in a thoughtful mood. What did I do wrong this time? What am I about to do wrong tomorrow?

Theory: every garden patch or field ought to have its own handbook passed down from generation to generation by those who have worked that particular plot of land. Every piece of land is different, every bit of ground is unique. Particularly in places like northern New Mexico, with its wide variation in soil profiles.

Beyond that we enter the arena of sometimes useful generalization. Until recent historical times, the most reliable horticultural lore lay in the minds of its innumerable practitioners. Of necessity most people lived on the land, or not far from it. And under the pressure of endless human tinkering, cultivated plant varieties evolved too quickly for agricultural writers and lumbering printing presses to keep up. Sound familiar? See growing things as the earth's software for which manuals can never quite keep pace. Rapid botanical change has been a constant feature of the cultivated plant world since the beginnings of domestication. What is new is the rising curve of recent accelerations in the form of developments like genetic engineering—and how such trends are passing the control of seed varieties away from countless individual growers to a handful of corporations.

A good rule may be: if you read it on paper, it's already out of date. But being a little behind the times in these matters may be a plus. In general you'll probably hear about it first—in a utilitarian way—from seed catalogues, which at their best are miniature encyclopedias. My current bible is the catalogue from Johnny's Selected Seeds of Albion, Maine. Their short-season, northern climate bias meshes well with the high altitude challenges of northern New Mexico, and their importation of the results of the latest Dutch and Japanese plant breeders is pegged to the needs of the market gardener (or chef gardener) living in this hotbed of gourmet cooks and upscale restaurants. For similar climatic reasons, I am also much taken by the catalogues of Bear Creek Narserics and Ronnigers' (potatoes, garlic, specialty onions) in Idaho.

There is one guide I came to late and somewhat to my surprise, given my envious confusion about the photographs of compulsively neat kitchens, gardens, and patios of the magazine: *The Sunset New Western Encyclopedia of Gardening*. The operative word here is *Western* in a publishing field dominated by Eastern and Southern gardening, in climates where rain appears from the sky on command.

Wendell Berry, Wes Jackson, Gary Nabhan, Annie Dillard, and Barry Lopez are household names, in households where there are books, and their volumes are on my shelves—because they help me become more attentive to what goes on in garden and field, and in the woods and along the river and acequias beyond. Berry and Nabhan work the land in one way or another, while Dillard and Lopez are keen observers of it.

For the larger Whys—of the Dust to Dust sort—I would take to a desert, or desertified, island three volumes, for understanding and consolation. One, Alice Attwater's elegant historical survey of the hydrology of North America, *Water*. Two, Wolfgang Sachs's (editor) *The Development Dictionary: Guide to Knowledge as Power*, an intellectual page-turner that helps explain why people sometimes prefer to remain masters of their fate by refusing to go along with current models of economic development that attempt to lure them away from the land. And, three, Clive Ponting's *An Ecological History of the World*, which explains what happens when people abuse directly and indirectly the land. His message is simple. Bad agricultural practices have brought most of the great civilizations to their knees. And ours is likely to be next.

For such thoughts, there is probably only one consolation: a spell of planting, weeding, and harvesting in the garden. Or just standing there, marveling at the wonder of it all.

|1994| Doubts about NAFTA, globalization, technological advances, and various economic schemes that promise a better life for all? Afraid to look our myriad social failures in the eye? Fearful of the future? Then *The Development Dictionary: A Guide to Knowledge as Power*[15] is the book for you.

The editor of this anthology, Wolfgang Sachs of the Wuppertal Institute in Germany, and his band of seventeen international cohorts gathered together in 1988 under the intellectual guidance of Ivan Illich to analyze the failure of forty years of economic development schemes concocted by the northern industrial nations to raise the "standard of living" of the former colonial territories of the southern hemisphere. An outgrowth of their meeting was *The Development Dictionary*. The somewhat metaphorical title refers to the alphabetical arrangement of its nineteen chapters, each headed by a key word of current economic thought: Development, Environment, Market, Participation, Planning, Population, and so on. The whole composes an intellectual page-turner of the highest order.

The term *underdevelopment* was coined by Harry Truman in a 1949 speech that kicked off development's hidden agenda, which was ". . . nothing else than the Westernization of the world."[16] It has run full tilt since then.

The cost? First of all the extinction of innumerable other ways of imagining, doing, creating, subsisting, speaking, and generally negotiating culturally within one's ecological means, which industrialism has never done and likely never will. Little examined in the public debate on such matters is the fact that the industrial north, in living so far beyond its means, can provide no example to the traditional societies it seeks to modernize and develop: "It has been estimated . . . that for the present world population to live at the per capita energy consumption level of the city of Los Angeles would require five planets."[17]

The problem is commonly construed as an excess of population and therefore an excess of poverty, while the painful reality may be that there is simply an excess of wealth, concentrated largely in the northern countries through centuries of colonial and now capitalist exploitation. In most matters, of course, we prefer to blame the victim. Lummis again: "A big part of the 'economic development,' i.e. the wealth, of the rich countries is wealth imported from the poor countries. The world economic system generates inequality and it runs on inequality."[18]

We are caught in this state of affairs, Otto Ullrich maintains in his essay on technology, because of the ". . . essential lie of the industrial system, the pretence that the material prosperity won through plundering and the transfer of costs was 'created' by industrial production, by science and technology. . . ."[19] We refuse to look squarely at the message of our trash cans, landfills, strip mines, clearcuts, and slums: "Perhaps the modern economy is essentially a way of organizing reality in a way that actually transforms both nature and people into waste."[20]

The first and foremost victims here are indigenous peoples and their languages and cultures, and their forests, waters, and landscapes. The long-term victim is diversity—cultural and biological—in all its forms, which is what differentiates this living sphere from the deadness of all moons. Science lends a willing hand in the degradation: "Nearly the entire coercive power of the modern state now comes from mega-science and mega-technology and developing the state today means primarily equipping it with greater coercive might as a result of the help of modern science and technology."[21] Working with planning and technology, science too has leveled and homogenized what was once rich and varied: "If one attempts to live close to the peasants or within the bosom of nature, modern science is perceived differently: as vicious, arrogant, politically powerful, wasteful, violent, unmindful of other ways."[22] Even environmental concerns, as Sachs points out in his essay "Environment," have been converted into opportunities for yet more planning, management, and exploitation on a global scale.

Northern New Mexico is as good a place as anywhere to look at the pathological effects of economic development: degraded rivers and streams, clearcut forests, stripmined mountains, an excess of wealth concentrated in Santa Fe and Los Alamos, cheek to jowl with some of the poorest counties in the nation, indigenous cultures pushed into marginalization, and a military death machine at the heart of it all.

For more details, for anyone attempting to imagine into existence a better future than the one officially mapped out for the globe, *The Development Dictionary* is an essential text.

|2000| We were talking about small scale agriculture in northern New Mexico, about water and traditional ace-quias, about the new Intel plant in Rio Rancho and about the new Wal-Mart in Española and the new Whole Foods store in Santa Fe. We were talking about how the next generation of small farmers can't afford to buy land within fifty miles of Santa Fe, where prices for irrigated bottom land start at $30,000 an acre. We were talking about the riots in Seattle over the World Trade Organization, which had just happened.

There were eight of us at the dinner table, all owners of parcels of irrigated land large enough to provide a living to some enterprising young farmer, and three of us small farm activists of one stripe or another. Until two years ago when I became a foundation grantee to develop a permanent farm-ers' market site in Santa Fe, my wife Rose Mary and I made a living (more or less) by growing garlic, onions, shallots on some seven acres fifty miles north of Santa Fe.

Our hostess, a commanding woman who loves to drop the cat among the pigeons, wrenched the conversation in a new direction and turned to me and asked: "Given your druthers, what would you like to see happen in the next ten years?" Re small farms, acequias, and farmers' markets in northern New Mexico.

During the rest of the evening I had no quick answer for my hostess's persistent demands for "a solution." Back at the farm, in bed, a thought came at 4:00 AM, an hour of reckoning when things seem either absurdly simple or impossibly complex. That particular AM, Simplicity raised its smiling head. "The world is upside down," it said, "so turn it rightside up."

Upside down? In agriculture, large corporate producers can outprice small producers because they don't have to factor in the costs of pollution, soil loss, health effects of pesticides and herbicides and nitrated-up groundwater, fossil fuel depletions, full benefits for farm laborers, and the withering away of village and small town infrastructures everywhere. Upside down? If you want to do the right thing and become a certified organic grower, you have to *pay* to use the word. As things now stand, you don't have to pay high taxes to poison the land or diminish the gene pool.

Rightside up would be to pay the full cost of these items, and to have them reflected in the cost of food. This is the point that Paul Hawken and Amory and L. Hunter Lovins make in *Natural Capitalism*.[23] Agriculture is our greatest source of pollution. When such costs are finally paid for by the producers and no longer by the taxpayer, then the cost of agribusiness-produced food will reflect the realities of monstrous feedlots, manure lagoons, and a billion pounds a year of herbicides and pesticides spread across the land. And then, rightside up, guess what: organic crops produced by small farms will not only be cheaper than agribusiness food, but organic products will be, as they have always been, better tasting, more nutritious, and healthier for everybody who has anything to do with them up and down the food chain. Take away all those subsidies that agribusiness has been destroying the world with and give them to small organic producers who are doing things the right way and then you will see your small farmer outbidding developers for farmland and water rights, even in northern New Mexico, and pushing city limits back to where they belong. Presto, everything is rightside up again.

Northern New Mexico is a fertile place for such thinking. The infrastructure of small-scale farming is still largely in place. There is land, water, and there are still feed stores and farm equipment dealers—and there are still farmers on the land. Northern New Mexico has the feel that it is still more or less rightside up.

But the dinner table conversation suggested that the world is about to flip over. If allowed to continue, unregulated development will soon fill the irrigated acres of our small river valleys with mobile homes, retirement homes, and second homes. The anarchistic acequia system made up of a thousand acequias governed by Spanish water law with roots in Moorish North Africa is under siege by well organized and financed commercial and municipal interests. Big box stores are moving into Santa Fe and Española at the rate of about one every two months, and the twenty-mile highway connecting the two will be an endless construction zone for the next several years. Northern New Mexico soon promises to be Upside Down just like everywhere else, distinguished from Everywhere Else only by its scenic backdrop of the Sangre de Cristo Range and its fake adobe architecture.

Development has come relatively slowly to northern New Mexico because of what was so well rooted here before. The Indian Pueblos have been particularly adept at ducking beneath the waves of cultural invasion, the first one Spanish, the second one Anglo. For centuries, the isolation of small Hispanic villages all over Northern New Mexico protected them from rapid assimilation into American ways. Against all odds, acequia traditions have remained strong in the small river valleys where subsistence farming and livestock production were once the center of village life. Acequia activists have always provided the ground troops to fight large-scale irrigation projects that would pry water management out of local hands, where it has been since Spanish colonists grafted a remarkably democratic water management tradition on to Pueblo Indian ways.

In the 1960s, acequias were made "bodies politic, subdivisions of the state," confirming what they had always been, the smallest entities of government in the country.

In the north, acequia activists have stymied large-scale water projects and transfers for the last generation, including the Pot Creek and Indian Camp Dam project near Taos (which provided fodder for John Nichols's *Milagro Beanfield War*), the Velarde Canal project, and the Rio Grande Phreatophyte Eradication Program. This last, an early 1980s brainwave, sought to clearcut 150 miles worth of Rio Grande cottonwoods from San Juan Pueblo south to Socorro, the better to fill the dams of southern New Mexico.

Acequias have proven to be an almost insurmountable barrier to the adjudication of water rights, a process by which Spanish water law, which binds land and water together, is replaced by American water law, which separates land from water, allowing water to "flow uphill to money" so that it can fuel municipal-industrial development. Acequias are an element in the legal tangles of the Aamodt water adjudication suit, which seeks to establish water claims in the Nambé, Pojoaque, and San Ildefonso area between Santa Fe and Española. Aamodt is the oldest case in the federal docket. Several years ago the case was estimated to be costing about $10,000 an irrigated acre, money that has gone not into rural infrastructure but into the hands of urban lawyers, surveyors, hydrologists, and bureaucrats.

The emergence of farmers' markets in the early 1970s in Los Alamos, Santa Fe, and Taos encouraged a whole new generation of small farmers to stay on the land—or return to it and to the water that is still in the acequias to irrigate their fields. Like farmers' markets everywhere, New Mexico's are based in a form of protectionism, in the rule that you sell only what you grow, and that your farm be within a certain region, assuring a very high degree of local content. In terms of global trade, this rule is probably in violation of some fine print clause in GATT or NAFTA. A detail, you might argue, but there are now twenty-eight farmers' markets in New Mexico alone, and five thousand nationally. And they have become recognized forces in downtown revitalization and farmland preservation everywhere.

Turning the world rightside up by getting the big boys to do the right thing is—conceptually—easy. The harder part lies in how to encourage the little fellow to do his part. Our dinner table conversation raked over the agonizing problem of how to encourage people to keep farming when they couldn't afford to buy land, when they had no access to long term credit to capitalize their operations, when they couldn't earn equity in rented land, when they had to work 16 hours a day during three seasons of the year, all for little money and virtually no fringe benefits. But these problems are all the negative side of large producers being able pass their environmental and social costs on to the public, of creating a playing field deeply tilted to favor the large and multinational and to marginalize the small and local.

What I would propose—until the big corporations clean up their act—is to create Local Content Zones in which local producers of all sorts but primarily farmers are protected from competition outside their self-determined region. A Local Content Zone could be anything from a farmers' market, a public market hall (several of which I recently visited in Baltimore), or even a small zone within a city, such as the soon to be developed city-owned Railyard property in downtown Santa Fe. Local Content Zones and their producers would be subsidized in exactly the same measure and degree as multinational producers are now subsidized. In other words, add up all the environmental and social costs not being covered in the cost of goods being produced and pass this amount on (by way of subsidy) to the Local Content Zones and their producers, which will enable them to start underpricing their multinational competition right away. This is just the sort of calculation the World Trade Organization should be able to do in a snap of the fingers.

In ten or twenty years, when the world turns rightside up—as increasingly acute environmental crises will force it to do, perhaps far too late—then subsidies to Local Content Zones can wither away, because our small locally based producers will be able to stand on their own two feet, on a finally leveled playing field—and one that is environmentally and socially accountable and responsible.

There will be those who argue that with subsidies you can make anything work. Exactly: our Upside Down World is a prime example.

1. Their *New Mexico Business Opportunity News* has evolved into *Designer/Builder Magazine*, a nationally distributed journal of socially responsible and ecological architecture and planning.

2. His *Cidermaster of the Río Oscuro* was published by the University of Utah Press in 2000.

3. Sanbusco, no saint, is a contraction of "Santa Fe Builders Supply Company."

4. It went out of business in 1998.

5. Until January 1998.

6. *Mayordomo: Chronicle of an Acequia in Northern New Mexico* covers a year in the life of the acequia, 1985–86; it was published by UNM Press in 1988.

7. Truman drove to the market well into his eighties and then was driven by family members to his last markets. The very last Saturday he attended, he sat hunched over in the cab of his pickup. He died the next day.

8. Acequias which band together to form watershed associations have since become eligible for funding from the State Engineer Office.

9. This invasive species is being appropriately eradicated in the Bosque del Apache Wildlife Preserve south of Socorro and other places along the Rio Grande.

10. This is not to say that the Rio Grande maintains a healthy riparian environment. Irrigation projects have curtailed the flooding necessary for cottonwoods to establish new colonies, leaving growths of grand old water-guzzling trees without offspring.

11. Fred Waltz has since moved into a private practice dealing with water issues, but under a Ford Foundation grant Legal Services was able to hire David Benividez, who has gradually established himself as an authority in water adjudication in relation to acequias and rural communities.

12. The Hammetts misplaced the tape.

13. As of 2002, the Aamodt suit remains unresolved.

14. No funding was appropriated for the commission. As of this writing, the most active advocacy groups for acequias are the non-profit Taos Valley Acequia Association, Chama Valley Acequia Association, and the New Mexico Acequia Association.

15. London and New Jersey: Zed Books, 1992.

16. Sachs, pp. 3–4.

17. "Equality," C.Douglas Lummis, p. 46. A few planets should be added to account for increase in northern consumption and southern population since 1988.

18. Op. cit., Lummis p. 46.

19. P. 280.

20. "Production," by Jean Roberts, p. 187.

21. "State," Ashis Nandy, p. 270.

22. "Science," Clade Alvares, p. 232.

23. Little, Brown and Compay; New York: 1999.